TURNAROUND

TURN-AROUND

THIRD WORLD LESSONS
FOR FIRST WORLD GROWTH

Peter Blair Henry

BASIC BOOKS
A MEMBER OF THE PERSEUS BOOKS GROUP
New York

Published by Basic Books,
A Member of the Perseus Books Group

Books published by Basic Books are available at special discounts for bulk
purchases in the United States by corporations, institutions, and other
organizations. For more information, please contact the Special Markets
Department at the Perseus Books Group, 2300 Chestnut Street, Suite 200,
Philadelphia, PA 19103, or call (800) 810-4145, ext. 5000, or e-mail
special.markets@perseusbooks.com.

Designed by Cynthia Young

Library of Congress Cataloging-in-Publication Data
Henry, Peter Blair.
Turnaround : third world lessons for first world growth / Peter Blair Henry.
    pages cm
Includes bibliographical references and index.
ISBN 978-0-465-03189-4 (hbk. : alk. paper)—ISBN 978-0-465-03191-7
(e-book)   1. Developing countries—Economic policy.   2. Capital movements—
Developing countries.   3. Capital market—Developing countries.   4. Debt
relief—Developing countries.   I. Title.
HC59.7.H4286 2013
338.9—dc23
                                                                    2012044337

10   9   8   7   6   5   4   3   2   1

For George Arthur Henry

CONTENTS

INTRODUCTION

TIMES HAVE CHANGED. CHINA NOW HAS THE SECOND-LARGEST economy in the world. Mexico, following almost twenty years of economic stability, now boasts 1.9 million manufacturing jobs, thriving innovation centers, and a burgeoning high-tech industry. Between 2001 and 2011, Brazil lifted 20 million people out of poverty and into its growing middle class, and in the last quarter of the twentieth century Botswana's gross domestic product per capita grew faster than that of any other country on the planet. The once-labeled "Third World" is edging its way into the "First World." Add to these observations the recent debt and financial crises that have battered the United States and Europe, and it becomes clear that the future prosperity of the global economy depends as never before on sustained growth in emerging markets as well as on the stabilization of our own shaky ground. Interdependence is paramount. In the years ahead, everyone will win or everyone will lose, and the outcome hinges critically on whether advanced nations muster the humility required to absorb and embrace the Third World's lessons for First World growth.

How did we arrive at this reversal of fortune? Not so long ago China seemed hopelessly mired in poverty, Mexico triggered the Third World Debt Crisis, and Brazil experienced one of the world's highest rates of inflation. How did these countries, and many others like them, engineer such a stunning economic turnaround? The answer, in a word, is discipline. Just as an individual's ability to delay gratification at a young age is a powerful predictor of future academic and professional achievement, discipline is also central to the long-run economic health of nations. The point sounds almost too obvious to state, but the definition of "discipline" that emerges from a historical analysis of the Third World's remarkable transformation may take you by surprise.

In the current economic and political climate, pundits and policymakers of all stripes erroneously equate discipline with possessing the courage to adopt extreme measures. In the fiscal debate raging across the United States and Europe, British prime minister David Cameron and German chancellor Angela Merkel assert that austerity now—massive deficit reduction—is the way to get advanced economies back on track, while Nobel Prize–winning economist Paul Krugman argues that governments need to maintain deficit spending until robust growth resumes. A government decision that slashes spending at the wrong time and sends a weak economy into a tailspin can be just as undisciplined as one that unleashes a wasteful spending spree in an overheated environment. Discipline does not call for crash diets or binge eating, but rather for healthy habits practiced consistently over a lifetime.

Discipline occasionally calls for extraordinary measures, but most of the time discretion is the better part of valor. Good economic policy requires not so much the bravado to implement drastic change as the strength and wisdom to make reasonable trade-offs over the many years it takes to transform a country's standard of living. Discipline in this context means self-control and a sustained commitment to the future, resisting the temptation to adopt policies that tilt entirely in one ideological direction or another and opting instead for the vigilant pursuit of a pragmatic middle road to prosperity.

Discipline also has a certain periodicity. Fluctuating across time and location, it is not an inherent trait forever present in some countries and permanently absent from others. Germany, a country that many people view as the epitome of self-control, printed radically large quantities of money during the 1920s, plunging the nation into

Setting aside personal proclivities isn't easy. I spent much of my childhood in the developing world, witnessing children begging on the street, and I devoted my young adulthood to the task of trying to figure out how to help poor countries prosper. As a doctoral student in the MIT economics department in the mid-1990s, I realized that an objective tool was already at hand for evaluating competing and emotionally charged claims about the likely future impact of changes in economic policy. Ironically, the answer for how best to understand what works for the poor turned out to be the stock market—a quintessential symbol of the rich.

Stock market reactions to economic reforms provide powerful forecasts of policy efficiency because they capture what author James Surowiecki calls "the wisdom of crowds."[2] Changes in the value of stocks reflect the average opinion of thousands of shareholders who do not care about ideological debates but simply want to know whether a given policy change will create or destroy economic value. Their collective assessment, as reflected in the national stock market index, is more reliable than the judgment of any individual.

But really, how wise is the crowd? Given the turbulence in financial markets since August 2007, it may seem like the height of either arrogance or ignorance to claim that the stock market is a reliable indicator of anything real. From Charles Kindleberger's classic work on financial crises, *Manias, Panics, and Crashes,* to the burgeoning field of behavioral economics, there is a lot of evidence that the market does not always reflect the true underlying value of stocks, let alone anything useful about the broader economy.

In his book *Irrational Exuberance,* Robert Shiller provides a number of examples of large stock price increases that were out of sync and apparently not triggered by any significant economic news. But the observation that stock prices sometimes fluctuate for no apparent reason does not mean that all stock price movements are uninformative. Indeed, Shiller himself candidly states that "some substantial fraction of the volatility in financial markets is probably justified by news about future dividends or earnings."[3]

In order to believe that the stock market has something useful to say about economic reforms, you do not have to accept the premise that stock prices are always spot on. All you need to acknowledge is that prices respond to significant revelations about a country's economy and that this will be the case as long as shareholders (current or prospective) seek to maximize their profits.[4] This is not an article of faith but a fact—especially in emerging markets, where the economic changes over the past three decades have been large and unprecedented.

So while it is true that the stock market sometimes gets out of step with the greater economy, competition ensures that the market does respond to major changes in policy, and the market's response is an objective and reliable, if imperfect, predictor of long-term economic impact.[5] Data show, for example, that in a wide range of developing countries shareholders drove up stock valuations fourfold in anticipation of various economic reforms enacted over a period of roughly three decades. Stock markets in the developing world predicted that reforms in those countries would improve their economic performance, and contrary to the increasingly popular view that the reform agenda failed to generate broad-based economic improvements, the markets were generally right.

Stock markets rose throughout the Third World because economic reforms, difficult as they were to implement, would eventually, if sustained, reduce inflation, open countries to the benefits of free trade, and make them more profitable places to do business. This begs the question: did stocks rise simply because the reforms signaled a political triumph of rich over poor that would result in a future redistribution of income from workers to shareholders? The facts indicate that the rise in valuations did more than create wealth for owners of shares. Higher stock prices reduced the cost of capital for firms, making it cheaper for them to invest in factories, equipment, and new technologies. Higher levels of investment increased the productivity, wages, and material well-being of workers in developing countries. In other words, the stock market served as both a useful predictor of whether changes in policy would have positive effects on the lives of people at all levels of society and a conduit through which those effects were actually transmitted. Reviewing developing countries' historical struggle with economic reform through the lens of their stock exchanges leaves little doubt that governments (in both the First and Third Worlds) in search of a growth strategy should go shopping in the store of market-friendly policies.

Although there is no single path to prosperity and all countries have to find their own way, one common thread leaps out from the evidence: discipline. Governments that adopt and maintain market-friendly reforms can deliver ongoing improvements to the material well-being of their people. Leaders who take shortcuts may produce abundance for a day but ultimately impoverish the masses. Discipline does not reside in the world of command-and-control economies; it also does not embrace extreme forms of laissez-faire capitalism.

Instead, discipline is a sustained commitment to a pragmatic growth strategy, executed with a combination of temperance, vigilance, and flexibility that values the long-term prosperity of the entire population over the short-term enrichment of any particular group of individuals. The optimal blend of policies that makes up the growth strategy differs from place to place, but the various roads to riches—all of them long—are paved with a mix of free markets, judicious regulation, and government provision of public goods like education, infrastructure, and health.

The stock market ultimately rewards disciplined policies that create long-run value, but there are important limitations to what it can teach us. The market is a *leading* indicator: it provides a forecast about the likely future impact of changes in policy, not an evaluation of the outcomes that actually come to pass. The traditional way of measuring policy effectiveness assesses impact using *lagging* economic indicators such as growth and inflation that become available only after the policy has been implemented. Since people live on the wages and profits of economic outcomes, not forecasts, is it not better to look directly at whether inflation declined and growth increased after the implementation of reforms?

The truth is that we need both perspectives—before and after—because lagging indicators do not tell us whether reforms failed because of bad policies or lack of discipline. Some economic reforms will even reduce growth in the period immediately following implementation, with turnarounds in performance coming only after years of sustained application. If a country abandons reform because the initial fall in growth proves unpopular with the populace, then it will seem as though the restructuring was bad for the economy when the truth is that growth would have been higher in the long run had the reforms been given a chance to work.

In contrast to lagging indicators, the market's reaction to the prospect of reform inherently takes into account the impact that market participants expect the policy change to have in both the short run and the long run. Accordingly, the stock market provides a powerful, non-ideological indicator of likely policy effectiveness and an important complement to traditional measures such as growth, inflation, and productivity—all of which we will continue to use throughout the book because they provide important reality checks.

Of course, where stock markets do not exist, we cannot use them to directly predict the impact of changes in policy. Since the former Soviet Union and much of Eastern Europe established stock markets at the same time they implemented their "shock therapy" free-market reforms, countries such as the Czech Republic, Poland, and Russia do not play a direct role in our story here. On the other hand, studying emerging economies for which the appropriate stock market data are available teaches us important lessons about the conditions under which shock therapy is likely to succeed and provides useful information to countries contemplating such an approach to their economic problems, now or in the future.

Replacing wasteful policies with efficient ones creates value for society, but it also produces winners and losers. The issue of how to treat the losers fairly is a multifaceted problem. First, there is the question of fairness within a given country undertaking reform. Efficient policies increase the size of the economic pie, and in principle everyone in the country, from workers to shareholders, can have a larger slice, but this is not a given in all cases. The path to greater efficiency can be painful and uneven. Opening up to free trade is a good example of a reform that raises national living standards over time but may exact a wrenching toll along the way: inefficient industries close, workers lose their jobs, and people must adjust to a different way of life as capital moves to newly profitable sectors of the economy and creates the employment of the future.

The challenge for leadership is to recognize the potential benefits of reform, make the disciplined decisions, and chart a course that allows what is good for the country as a whole to prevail over the preferences of corporations, unions, candidates for public office, or any other group that would forestall national progress to protect its own narrow interests. Where appropriate, it also makes sense to provide a safety net for the losers—both on humanitarian grounds and because ameliorating the unequal impact of change may increase the likelihood of sustaining reforms over time.

Sustaining the benefits of reform also requires attention to issues of fairness in international relations. In an interdependent world, relationships between countries have an impact on policies, and policies between countries affect whether companies make profits and people have jobs. Fairness in the context of international relations is not just about good manners; it's a matter of good business. Viewed through that lens, the developed world's treatment of its newly prosperous colleagues around the globe is of particular concern. For the past three decades, developed countries have used their leverage at international institutions like the IMF, the World Bank, and the World Trade Organization (WTO) to lecture the developing world about the good things that would happen to their economies if they reduced inflation, liberalized trade, and privatized state-owned enterprises.

Again, after many fits and starts, and in some cases at great political cost, a number of developing countries found the discipline to implement and sustain key parts of the reform agenda. Because of their newfound commitment to the future, the growth rate of developing countries surged after 1995, and their output now accounts for almost 50 percent of global economic activity. In spite of this fact, the developing world receives short shrift in the realm of international economic relations. The voice and representation of developing countries at multilateral institutions pale in comparison to their contributions to the world economy. The WTO has failed to secure a global trade deal that provides equal access to global markets for emerging countries, and no citizen of the developing world has ever been chosen to lead the IMF or the World Bank. To make matters worse, the challenging economic outlook tempts governments of advanced countries to look inward, to adopt various forms of protectionism, and to pursue growth strategies eerily reminiscent of those they urged developing countries to abandon in the recent past.

Why does this response from the First World and the continued marginalization of the Third World matter so much? For a variety of reasons related to the ways in which developed-country governments pushed the economic reform agenda and now fail to acknowledge the success of their counterparts in the developing world, voters and policymakers in emerging economies are suffering from "reform fatigue." A recent survey of seventeen Latin American nations found that only 18 percent of respondents thought that a market economy was good for their country.[6] Because further reforms are vital for continued and even more rapid growth in the emerging world, all countries—advanced and advancing—will be losers if reform fatigue sets in permanently and begins to spread. Developing-market growth alone cannot save the world economy, but rapidly expanding emerging economies and their burgeoning middle classes will buy more exports from the advanced world, help put its unemployed labor forces back to work, and blow vital wind into the sails of the developed world's beleaguered economic ship.

Thanks to the steady accumulation of disciplined policy choices by a number of developing countries, a major revision of "Who's Who in the World Economy" has taken place, with more disruption yet to come. Will officials in Washington, London, Brussels, and beyond embrace this shift, recognize the accomplishments of developing countries, and invite them into a new dialogue about the future of the world economy on terms commensurate with their importance to the global marketplace? Or will leaders of rich nations continue to resist the tide, insisting on a Pyrrhic victory that preserves their economic hegemony even as it undermines their (and everyone else's) future standard of living? As evidenced by the 2008 collapse of the WTO's Doha Development Round of negotiations with developing countries and the unrealized gains of potential free trade agreements, everybody loses without cooperation and consensus. Ironically, whether the emerging world continues to make policy choices that will contribute to shared prosperity for all nations hangs critically on whether the First World, now facing its own mountain of challenges, avoids the temptation to see prosperity as a zero-sum game and instead adopts the humility and discipline it needs to internalize the Third World economic lessons that lie in the pages ahead.

PART ONE

CHAPTER 1

Miss Mama

GROWING UP AS A LITTLE BOY ON THE ISLAND OF JAMAICA IN
the early 1970s, I cherished the time I spent on the porch of my
grandmother's simple two-bedroom ranch house in Kingston, the nation's capital. There, at Three Windy Way in Harbour View, a middle-
and working-class neighborhood at the southern edge of the city, I
would sit on the brown, speckled tile, leafing through the pages of *En-
cyclopaedia Britannica,* reading Bible stories, and poring over back issues of *National Geographic* for hours on end. As sea breezes stirred
the needles of the casuarina trees that lined the front yard and shaded
my world from both the sun and the gazes of people passing by on the
sidewalk, scents from Grandma's kitchen—pumpkin soup, baking
bread, brown sugar, and lime juice—wafted through the air.

Things only got better as the day progressed and the sun made its
arc through the cobalt expanse of the Jamaican afternoon sky. The
approach of evening was always my favorite stretch of time—a
welcome pause between the heat of day and the fall of darkness.
Grandma, finished with her cooking and housework, would come
outside and sit with me in the early evening air. Encouraging children to read and dream was what Grandma, a former schoolteacher,
did best, and she never missed an opportunity to work with one of
her favorite students. Sitting together in the fading light, we lost

ourselves in conversation, accompanied by the pulse of chirping crickets, the reverberating reggae beats from a nearby rum shop, and the animated voices of young men playing soccer in the street. These are the sounds of the Caribbean, the lyrical backdrop to Grandma's outdoor classroom, where I asked question after question about the people and places I had encountered in the day's reading and my ever-patient teacher shared with me facts and figures about distant lands.

Yet the greatest lesson I learned from my grandmother came not from something she read to me but from something she did for someone else. In Jamaica, as in many developing countries, poverty is never far away. On one occasion, the ambient sounds of those Caribbean evenings gave way to the piercing call of a woman at the front gate: "Mrs. Henry! Mrs. Henry, you deh so? Me beg you mek me come in."

When poverty calls to you from the gate, you have to make a choice. You can avert your eyes, perhaps even turn your back and harden your resolve not to engage, but poverty will still be there looking at you, even if you don't have the courage to return its gaze.

"Soon come," Grandma called out as she lifted her tiny, slightly hunched frame from the chair next to me, walked across the tiles, stepped from porch to carport, and made the thirty-foot journey to the gate. "Good evening, Miss Mama. How are you?"

Miss Mama's appearance belied her reply, "Me all right so far, Mrs. Henry." Miss Mama looked anything but "all right" to me as I watched her follow Grandma toward the porch. The closer Miss Mama came to my sacred classroom, the sharper the contrast I discerned between her and my beloved tutor. With bare feet, tattered clothes, matted hair, and a protruding belly seemingly at odds with her thin frame, Miss Mama appeared to be from an entirely different planet than my grandmother, who, with her pressed and starched cotton dress and neatly groomed appearance, was the quintessential schoolteacher and matron of the Anglican Church.

After inviting Miss Mama to sit down next to her (and across from me), Grandma asked Miss Mama if she was hungry. Miss Mama replied, "Yes, Mrs. Henry. Is long time me nah eat you know, maam." My grandmother disappeared inside, then emerged a few minutes later with a large tumbler of milk and a plate of warm, hard dough bread, dripping with butter. I sat there, watching Miss Mama eat and listening to the exchange—my grandmother asking questions in the Queen's English, Miss Mama responding in patois.

They continued on for some time—Miss Mama chronicling her tough circumstances, my grandmother offering words of comfort and encouragement—until the last crumbs disappeared from the plate, the milk was drained, and my grandmother sent Miss Mama on her way with the familiar Jamaican benediction, "Walk good."

I don't know how Miss Mama got her name, and I don't know where she came from, but I can picture her today just as I saw her in that first encounter in late 1977 when I was eight years old. Over the next several months, Miss Mama appeared at my grandmother's front gate with increasing frequency. One day in 1978, following what turned out to be the last time I saw Miss Mama, I asked my grandmother: "Grandma, Miss Mama has a big belly, so why is she always hungry?" My grandmother replied that some people have big bellies not from eating too much but because they never get enough to eat.

For me, economics is all about Miss Mama. I was drawn to the subject because I wanted to help people in developing countries like my native Jamaica help themselves. Feeding the hungry is an act of kindness. Providing the hungry with the means to feed themselves is an act of empowerment that confers dignity as well as nourishment. My grandmother was too old and lacked the technical training to give people like Miss Mama that kind of enabling assistance. I wrote this book because I have no such excuse.

Helping people to help themselves begins with a simple observation. Never in the history of the world has a country sustainably reduced poverty without significantly increasing its population's average overall standard of living. The gains from economic expansion may not be evenly distributed, so growth alone is not a sufficient condition for development. But it is absolutely necessary. Without growth, life becomes a series of zero-sum struggles directed at preserving one's share of limited resources. With growth, the pie expands and the politics of distribution no longer involve such stark trade-offs. Because economic expansion provides the most reliable means of enabling the poor to lift themselves out of poverty, the critical question is: what kinds of economic policies lay the foundation for growth?

The economic policy decisions implemented in the months and years ahead will determine whether people eat or starve, live or die—and not just in emerging economies. The financial crisis of 2008–2009 drove record numbers of people in the United States into unemployment, foreclosure, and poverty, to say nothing of the devastating impact of its aftershocks on the economies and people of Europe. Whether in the First World or the Third, there is no place to hide from the power of policy.

As with so many things in life, gaining a useful perspective on the right way to move forward requires a careful look back.

From Kingston to Korea

At the same time Miss Mama was recounting her hardscrabble life in Kingston in the 1970s, an unprecedented lending boom was under way in the wider developing world. Commercial banks in London, New York, and Tokyo freely lent money to developing-country governments from Manila to Mexico City. National officials used much of that money to fund a strategy for economic growth based on something called "dependency theory," the dominant intellectual paradigm in the developing world at the time, especially in Latin America.

An intellectual descendant of the Marxist school of thought, dependency theory argued that developing countries—"the periphery"—were poor because of a historically unequal set of power relationships with developed countries—"the center"—that kept the people of the periphery dependent on the center for high-value manufactured goods like cars and refrigerators and relegated them to working in low-value, low-wage industries like bananas and sugar. According to dependency theory, if poor countries wanted to break this cycle of dependency and one day become rich, they needed to abandon the thinking that drove economic policymaking in the capitals of the center and employ an alternative model of economic development.

For instance, instead of relying on international trade and free markets as engines of growth, dependency theory encouraged developing-country governments to pursue a policy of "import substitution." As the term implies, import substitution called for a country's manufacturing sector to develop the capability and expertise to produce locally those goods that the country had previously imported from abroad. Because many domestic manufacturers were starting from scratch and thus would be less efficient than their foreign counterparts, import substitution advocated government support for them in the form of financial subsidies plus tariffs and/or outright restrictions on the quantity of foreign imports allowed to enter the country. Proponents of dependency theory believed that import substitution would empower developing countries to change their traditional patterns of trade with developed countries, help them become more self-reliant, and accelerate their path to prosperity. Coming as it did on the heels of the Third World independence movement, dependency theory had particularly strong appeal in Africa, Latin America, and parts of Asia that saw themselves as victims of neocolonialism.

While loans were plentiful in the 1970s, developing countries vigorously pursued import substitution and various other policies inspired by dependency theory. By the beginning of the next decade, however, signs had begun to emerge that all was not well. Investment of the borrowed money in unprofitable domestic industries, rising world interest rates, and a global recession had all combined to substantially reduce the value of the international banks' loan portfolios in the debtor countries. As the current and future economic prospects of the debtors dimmed, the banks rushed to call in their loans. New lending ground to a standstill, and the short-term payment burden for the debtors became unmanageable.

In the absence of new lending, scarce resources that would normally have funded investment in developing countries were consumed by debt servicing. Countries had to choose between balancing their budgets or continuing to run deficits and financing them by printing money (also known as "monetizing" the deficit). Many countries chose the latter option. As the difference between expenditures and revenues grew, governments, cut off from external creditors, relied ever more heavily on printing money to meet their fiscal shortfalls. As a consequence, prices soared, currencies lost their value, and inflation crises ensued. Under these circumstances, life became particularly miserable for the poor. When faced with inflation, the wealthy can use financial markets to protect their assets, but the poor have limited access to financial services and find it hard to keep inflation from devouring the purchasing power of their already meager income and any savings they might have.

On August 12, 1982, Mexico defaulted on its external debt, marking the start of what came to be known as the "Third World Debt Crisis." Over the next three years, no fewer than forty countries in Asia, Africa, and Latin America, encompassing roughly 40 percent of the Third World, ran headlong into debt-servicing difficulties. Standards of living tumbled as gross domestic product per capita in the troubled countries contracted by 2.5 percent in 1982, 4.8 percent in 1983, and an average of 1.6 percent per year from 1982 through 1985.[1] As incomes fell, social unrest boiled over and protesters took to the streets in Argentina, Bolivia, Brazil, Ecuador, Mexico, and many other countries. Just as the European debt saga today raises fears that a default by Italy or Spain will trigger a repeat of the 2008–2009 financial crisis, in the early 1980s bankers and public officials worried that defaults by large borrowers such as Mexico and Brazil would cause a collapse of the international banking system.

With developing countries teetering near the abyss and threatening to take the advanced nations down with them, global financial stability was certainly on the line. But something even bigger was at stake. The mid-1980s marked the height of the Cold War and the battle of ideas that would shape the future course of the world: Ronald Reagan and Margaret Thatcher against Mikhail Gorbachev and the "Evil Empire," or the power of markets versus the power of the command economy. In this context, the Third World Debt Crisis presented an opportunity for one of the world's two great superpowers at the time to exert its intellectual hegemony. On October 8, 1985, US Secretary of the Treasury James A. Baker III gave a speech in Seoul, South Korea, that did just that. Baker's speech, delivered at the annual meetings of the International Monetary Fund and the World Bank Group, outlined a three-point "Program for Sustained Growth" (known thereafter as "the Baker Plan"). In the words of Baker's boss, President Reagan, the program was designed to "address problems of debt and declining growth in developing countries."[2]

The problem, as Baker outlined it, was low growth and wasteful spending as a result of years of adherence to dependency theory and its philosophy of closed markets and extensive state intervention in the economy. In his view, the only way out was for the countries in question to commit to macroeconomic reforms such as inflation stabilization, trade liberalization, privatization, and freer flows of capital.[3] These reforms would pave the road to increased prosperity for developing countries. In return for adopting these reforms, the US Treasury, the International Monetary Fund (IMF), the World Bank, and other multilateral financial institutions pledged to lend developing countries the money they needed to meet their debt obligations, restructure their economies, and renew their relationships with the capital markets.

The Baker Plan did not resolve the debt crisis—that distinction would go to the Brady Plan set forth four years later by Baker's successor, Nicholas F. Brady. In time, the Brady Plan would consolidate the process of reform, relieve some of the debt burden, and restore developing-country access to private credit markets. But the Baker Plan did send an unambiguous signal with broad ramifications. In calling for stabilization, liberalization, and privatization, Baker delineated in no uncertain terms the intellectual framework that would drive the official US position on economic policy in developing countries for the rest of the Reagan presidency and beyond. The message, to put it mildly, was not well received.

THE WASHINGTON CONSENSUS FIGHT

In the aftermath of Baker's speech, policymakers, the general populace, and even economists in developing countries publicly railed against the call for a sea change in their economic policies, accusing the unholy trinity of the US Treasury, the IMF, and the World Bank of forcing a "neocolonial" agenda down the throats of developing nations that had no choice but to succumb to the ideologically driven US demands or else become pariahs of the international capital market. The accusations came in many forms, but all were variations on a basic theme: the international financial orthodoxy pushed Third World governments to adopt policies that hurt the poor and were generally not in the economic interest of anyone except the banks that had lent money to the developing countries.

In 1989 economist John Williamson tried to take the debate out of the ideological realm. In an article titled "What Washington Means by Policy Reform," he coined the term "Washington Consensus" as a convenient shorthand expression for the set of ten policies, outlined in Baker's speech, that the US Treasury, the IMF, and the World Bank thought were useful instruments for achieving the economic objectives of high growth, low inflation, sustainable finances, and an equitable distribution of income.

THE TEN ORIGINAL WASHINGTON CONSENSUS POLICIES

1. Fiscal discipline
2. Reorientation of public expenditures
3. Tax reform
4. Financial liberalization
5. Unified and competitive exchange rates
6. Trade liberalization
7. Openness to foreign direct investment
8. Privatization
9. Deregulation
10. Secure property rights[4]

Williamson emphasized that irrespective of whatever intellectual worldview Washington wanted to push, the ten policy instruments on the list were not desirable for their own sake. Rather, the essential point was that some subset of the list of instruments would provide the most efficient means for developing countries to achieve the goal of greater and sustainable economic prosperity.

Instead of taking Williamson's narrow, rather clinical construction in the spirit with which it was offered, however, many interested observers misappropriated the term "Washington Consensus" and used it as shorthand for a broader agenda of small government, elimination of the welfare state, and other political goals outside the realm of economic efficiency. With the fall of the former Soviet Union in the late 1980s, the term "Washington Consensus" became an "ill-suited and temporary substitute for the all-encompassing ideological frameworks that millions of people had come to depend on to shape their opinions about affairs at home and abroad, judge public policies, and even steer some aspects of their daily lives."[5] Given the infusion of the term with ideology and meaning far beyond Williamson's original technocratic intent, it is not surprising that more than a decade later, in Williamson's own words, "there are people who cannot utter ['Washington Consensus'] without foaming at the mouth."[6]

The term "Washington Consensus" may evoke even greater controversy today than when it was first unveiled. More than a quarter-century after Baker's speech in Seoul, antiglobalization protesters gather every year at the annual meetings of the IMF and the World Bank to blame Consensus-driven policies for the economic divide between rich and poor nations. Building on anti-Consensus sentiment, Venezuelan president Hugo Chavez garnered political support and $7 billion of financial backing for the launch of Banco del Sur, a South American regional development bank that he sees as an alternative to the IMF, the World Bank, and their "failed imperialist agenda" that amounts to "the fundamental cause of the great evils and the great tragedies currently suffered."[7]

Although one may discount Chavez's statements as the ranting of an unapologetic left-wing ideologue, other scathing critiques of the Washington Consensus cannot be so readily dismissed because they come from observers who actually restrict their criticism to the specific economic policy reforms. One can find equally hard-line observers, however, who hold the opposite perspective. In general, then, there are two starkly differing views about the value to developing countries of the economic policy reform agenda pursued to varying degrees over the past three decades.

On the Left Side of the Ring . . . the Cynics

A series of books and articles by leading scholars lends credibility to the antireform camp from the highest ranks of academia. A year after winning the 2001 Nobel Prize in Economics, Joseph Stiglitz published a book that openly expressed his disgust with Washington's strident advocacy of economic reforms throughout the developing world.[8] Expressing his ongoing dismay at the promulgation of the reform agenda, Stiglitz wrote elsewhere at the time: "It seems perverse simultaneously to argue both for measures that enhance global volatility and against measures that enhance worker security. Yet this is precisely the position that advocates of the neoliberal doctrines have taken."[9]

In 2006 economist Dani Rodrik published a blistering polemic consigning the Washington Consensus to the dustbin of history. "Nobody really believes in the Washington Consensus anymore. The question is not whether the Washington Consensus is dead or alive; it is what will replace it." Rodrik went on to say, "The evidence that macroeconomic policies, price distortions, financial policies, and trade openness have predictable, robust, and systematic effects on national growth rates is quite weak."[10] In other words, the economic reform agenda failed.

ON THE RIGHT SIDE . . .
THE ADVOCATES

On March 23, 2004, Anne Krueger, first deputy managing director of the IMF from 2001 to 2006 and a longtime champion of economic reform in the developing world, delivered a roundtable lecture to the Economics Honor Society at New York University offering a perspective in diametric opposition to Rodrik's point of view. The title of Professor Krueger's lecture was not subtle: "Meant Well, Tried Little, Failed Much: Policy Reforms in Emerging Market Economies." Krueger made the case that, in spite of good intentions, economic reforms in most parts of Latin America and much of the developing world were not sufficiently ambitious and that governments lacked the commitment to see tough reforms through to completion.[11]

In a speech given a year earlier, Francisco Gil Díaz, the Mexican minister of finance at the time, expressed a view very close to Krueger's when he said, "The policies that have been undertaken [in Latin

America] are not even a pale imitation of what market economics ought to be, if we understand market economics as the necessary institutional framework for a sound economy to operate and flourish. What has been implemented throughout our continent is a grotesque caricature of market economics."[12] He cited the failure of Latin American leaders to vigorously pursue macroeconomic stability, free trade, and privatization as evidence of the region's unwillingness to embrace the policy changes needed to promote growth.

Said another way, advocates of economic reform argue that a lack of commitment by poor countries, particularly in Africa and Latin America, is what truly hinders their ability to close the income gap with rich nations. To paraphrase G. K. Chesterton, it is not that economic reforms have been tried and found wanting; it is that economic reforms have been found difficult and left untried.

And the Winner Is . . .

Should developing nations stay the course and persist with the hard work of deepening the economic reforms that many began implementing in the 1980s and 1990s? And if so, what are the implications for how the United States and Europe will deal with their deficit, debt, and unemployment problems? Given that the critical economic policy questions for advanced nations in the years ahead will bear an increasing resemblance to the Third World problems of the past, it is more important than ever to understand the true impact of economic reforms. The trouble is that even before the cataclysmic economic events of 2008–2009, it was hard to know which set of opinions about the impact of economic reform to trust. Now, in the aftermath of a once-in-a-lifetime crisis that many believe was caused by the very policies at the heart of the reform agenda, opinions have become increasingly divergent and entrenched, making it even harder to discern heat from light. Many people will choose to support one view or another on the basis of what confirms their personal biases. Others are swayed by what makes the evening news.

Credible periodicals, including some with established track records in support of the Washington Consensus, have suggested that the Great Recession of 2008–2009 has undermined the case for modern economic theory and capitalism more generally. In July 2009, *The Economist* ran an issue with a cover displaying a picture of a tome with the words "Modern Economic Theory" on it. The book was shown to be melting away, like so much ice. In August of the same year, *The Economist* published an article by Nobel Prize–winning economist Robert Lucas, who offered a stern rebuke to the sentiments and arguments put forth in the previous month's issue. Given two very different views of the world, how do we evaluate competing claims?

PRESENT VALUE

If you want to understand whether an economic policy change is likely to help or hurt a country's economy, then the response of that nation's stock market to the announcement of the change is about as unbiased an arbiter as you are likely to find. Stock prices reflect the average opinion of thousands of market participants. The stock market's forecast of whether a policy change will create or destroy value is more accurate than the opinion of any given business leader, economist, or policymaker.

Because the owner of a share of the national stock market index receives the cash payments that accrue to the underlying shares in perpetuity, she has great incentive to care about the performance of the economy not only today but indefinitely far into the future as well. This means that stock prices will respond to news about present and expected future cash flows and discount rates. Present and future cash flows drive the ability of companies to make payments to shareholders in the form of dividends and/or repurchases of shares and depend on the strength of the economy. Discount rates matter because a dollar of cash flow distributed today is worth more to shareholders than the expectation of a dollar to be paid out a year from now or even further down the road. The discount that shareholders apply to expected future cash payments depends on the levels of interest rates and risk in the economy. When interest rates go down, stock prices go up, and vice versa. Greater risk in the form of more uncertain future cash flows decreases stock prices; conversely, a reduction in risk is good for the market.

Readers steeped in finance will recognize that the preceding paragraph describes how stock prices represent the "present value" of the expected future cash payments associated with the underlying shares. For the lay reader, this means that stock prices are a weighted average of future payments to shareholders, where the weights depend on interest rates and risk—risk being not just a theoretical concept but an ambient reality in the daily lives of leaders around the world. And what leaders choose to do in the face of such uncertainty has profound long-run implications for the people who live in the countries they serve. The stock market gives us an educated forecast of the likely impact—the present value—of those decisions.

Using the stock market to assess the expected impact of reforms on an economy minimizes ideological differences and enables us to grapple objectively with some of the most important and controversial economic questions of our time: Is it possible to reduce inflation or otherwise stabilize an economy without undermining economic growth? Should countries permit capital to flow freely in and out of their economies? Is it efficient to relieve the financial obligations of nations that are in danger of defaulting on their debt? Essentially, if people expect a policy change to create value in a country undertaking reform, the stock price index will go up. Policies expected to destroy value will have the opposite effect.

The fact that stock markets throughout the emerging world have generally been right in their predictions that reforms would improve troubled economies does not imply that the Washington Consensus should become the "Decalogue of Economic Reform"—a list of ten policy changes to be implemented immediately and in their totality and to be adhered to without fail at all times. Rather, it suggests that when suffering from economic distress, developed and developing countries alike would do well to look to the world of fiscal temperance, monetary restraint, and open markets, choosing the necessary set of policies that best fit their individual circumstances and provide the biggest bang for the buck. The growth strategy that works for one country will not work for another because there will always be differences in local conditions—natural resources, culture, and politics, to name a few. What is critical to understand, however, is that every country that has made the transition from an emerging to a developed economy adopted at least some elements of the economic reform agenda—and did so in a disciplined manner.

Third World Lessons for First World Growth

Life takes strange turns. Ironically, more than three decades removed from my childhood in Jamaica, I find myself a proud citizen of a country wrestling with many of the same economic problems that plagued my native land. Battered banks, runaway government debt, high unemployment, and a seeming inability to resolve these problems have shaken confidence in the American dream. America is still the land of opportunity, but the litany of issues facing the country makes it impossible to escape the sense that something is wrong. In the words of an airport worker quoted by *Wall Street Journal* columnist Peggy Noonan, too many Americans have the sinking feeling that they are "out of Jobs [Steve], out of Hope [Bob], and out of Cash [Johnny]."[13] And as serious as they are, America's economic difficulties in 2012 look like child's play in comparison with the problems of its beleaguered European cousins.

At the time this book went to press, the European Union was on the brink of recession, Greek government bonds had been restructured, and the solvency of Portugal, Ireland, Italy, and Spain remained seriously in question. What began as a Greek cold became a full-fledged European flu with the potential to break up the euro currency zone. Hardly a news cycle seemed to go by without pictures of people taking to the streets to protest government plans for fiscal austerity and structural reforms.

The challenges facing the United States, Europe, and the rest of the developed world are immediately recognizable to people familiar with the trials of developing countries over the last several decades. Not surprisingly, then, the Third World's struggle with economic reform holds many important lessons for the First World as it contends with its own need for economic restructuring. The stories of economic turnaround in the developing world reveal how smart policies oriented toward long-term growth can propel a nation forward and provide a basis for the future prosperity of its citizens. The First World needs an ideas boost, and Third World nations can supply it. Indeed, the biggest unresolved question facing the global economy in the years ahead is not whether reforms help or hurt emerging economies, but whether policymakers in the capitals of developed countries— Washington in particular—will have the courage to practice what they have long preached.

Lessons for growth are not the only Third World message for the First World. From the parables of individual success in emerging markets comes a much larger moral. America and Europe have much to learn about humility, cooperation, and inclusion. As the emerging world continues to grow, its citizens, political leaders, and business leaders will continue to demand greater respect from and inclusion into Western economic and political institutions. Failure to adopt a more rational, meritocratic, and equitable approach will jeopardize the future prosperity of us all.

I have learned many things along the way from Kingston to New York, but none more important than the following lesson: the globalization of the world economy—that is, the interconnectedness of markets for goods, services, and capital—provides our greatest hope for helping people like Miss Mama lift themselves out of poverty, and economic reforms are a necessary (but not sufficient) condition for countries to take full advantage of globalization. If the facts in this book do not persuade you that this is the right lesson to draw from the economic experiences of the emerging world in the latter half of the twentieth century, then I hope that I am at least able to convince you of the value of my approach.

CHAPTER 2

POLICY MATTERS

"JAMAICA HAS NO ROOM FOR MILLIONAIRES," DECLARED
Prime Minister Michael Manley in 1975, expressing the view, common to many Third World leaders of the era, that the pursuit of individual wealth would undermine national economic development. For
those who wanted to be millionaires, Manley suggested, "We have five
flights a day to Miami."[1] Having chosen careers as scientists, my
mother and father did not consider getting rich a top priority, but the
prime minister's antibusiness stance produced unintended consequences that eventually forced them to take Manley's advice and put
our family on a one-way flight to the States.

Our family lived in a small rural village called Hampstead in the
Parish of St. Mary, the heart of Jamaica's cocoa-growing district. My
father formulated and supervised the manufacturing process for trans-
forming cocoa beans into chocolate for Cadbury Foods in the nearby
town of Highgate; Mom conducted research on cocoa and vegetable
pathology at an agricultural station called Orange River. In 1977
Cadbury Foods decided that the cost of doing business in Manley's
Jamaica was too high and moved its operations to West Africa. My father took another job in Kingston, but the one-hundred-mile round-
trip commute pitted the cost of gas against the cost of food for the
family. My mother's work environment also became increasingly

difficult as government restrictions on imports and a lack of funding combined to make obtaining appropriate research equipment and personnel a Herculean task. When it became apparent that our local school was going to close because of financial problems, my parents finally decided that moving to the United States with a family of six and few assets would give them a better chance of educating their children than soldiering on in a country in the midst of an economic free fall.

Sponsored by my twelve-year-old sister, who was born in Chicago when my parents were there completing their PhDs, our family drove to the US embassy in Kingston and stood in line with throngs of others trying to leave the island. We obtained the necessary emigration documents and left the country on February 28, 1978. Hard times require hard choices.

The move to the States quickly taught me two things. First, winter in Chicago is a lot colder than in Kingston. Second, our middle-class neighbors in the suburbs had a great deal more disposable income than middle-class families we knew in Jamaica, including ourselves. Furthermore, the streets of Wilmette were largely devoid of the poor, hungry, and homeless. The question of why standards of living are higher in some countries than in others is one of the great mysteries of economics. Understanding the causes of such disparity and searching for solutions has been my personal obsession in the more than thirty years since I arrived in the United States.

A Tale of Two Islands

Since at least the publication of Adam Smith's *The Wealth of Nations* in 1776, economists have known of the strong correlation between a country's economic performance and the nature of its institutions. Rich countries like the United States have laws that provide incentives for firms and entrepreneurs to engage in productive economic activity. Investors rely on secure property rights that encourage the accumulation of physical and human capital; government power is balanced and restricted by an independent judiciary; contracts are enforced effectively, supporting private economic transactions; and so on.

In their best-selling book of 2012, *Why Nations Fail,* Daron Acemoglu and James Robinson ostensibly demonstrate the definitive role of institutions in economic development. They compare countries whose colonizers established strong, constitutionally protected property rights hundreds of years ago (namely the British) with those whose colonizers did not.[2] They find that countries whose people were colonized by the British have much higher standards of living than countries colonized by the French or Spanish. In a similar vein, differences in the legal systems that countries inherited from their colonizers also have a major impact on long-run development. Countries with legal systems based on English common law provide investors with stronger protection and are less prone to government ownership and regulation than those with systems based on French civil law, which places weaker limitations on the power of the state. Consequently, English common law countries typically have greater financial development, less corruption, and lower unemployment.[3]

The "colonial origins" theory of development, or the "institutions are destiny" theory, has many adherents, but the part of the Caribbean in which I grew up provides a tale of two islands that throws cold water on this theory.[4] Barbados and Jamaica are both former British colonies. Jamaica gained independence in 1962, Barbados in 1966. As former colonies of the British Empire, the two countries inherited virtually identical institutions: the English language, Westminster parliamentary democracy, constitutional protection of private property, English common law, and the Anglican Church for good measure. These two tropical islands are predominantly inhabited and now governed by the descendants of West African slaves who were brought to the New World to cultivate sugar and other cash crops during the period of the "Transatlantic Triangular Trade" between Europe, Africa, and the Americas. In addition to their institutional, linguistic, geographic, and ethnic likenesses, both countries enjoy an abundance of sun, sand, and sea. Jamaica does have large deposits of bauxite—a key ingredient in the production of aluminum—whereas Barbados does not; however, this greater natural resource endowment actually deepens the following puzzle.

Starting from comparable standards of living in 1960, when GDP per capita was $3,395 US dollars in Barbados and $2,208 in Jamaica, and both nations fell under the World Bank's "Lower Middle Income" classification, the two countries experienced dramatically different outcomes. GDP per capita is now $14,998 in Barbados and $5,275 in Jamaica. In other words, the income gap between the two countries today is more than eight times larger than in 1960 and exceeds the total average level of income in Jamaica. Figure 2.1 shows that from 1960 through 2011 Barbados's GDP per capita grew twice as fast as Jamaica's—2.0 percent per year versus 1.0 percent per year—after adjusting for inflation.[5] The precipitous decline in Jamaica's standard of living that set in during the 1970s is particularly striking. From 1972 to 1987, Jamaica's economy contracted at a rate of 2.8 percent per year while Barbados's expanded by 1.5 percent. The vast difference in the countries' incomes today is largely a consequence of this fifteen-year period in which Barbados's growth rate exceeded Jamaica's by 4.3 percentage points per year.

How could this happen? Why did Barbados become so much richer than Jamaica following independence, in spite of all of their common characteristics? To understand this divergence of fortune, we need to look at the starkly contrasting set of economic policies pursued by the sovereign governments of Barbados and Jamaica within the same colonially inherited institutional framework. Leaders don't make policy decisions in a vacuum but rather in response to real-time events that present challenges to their goals and priorities. The lion's share of the income gap between Barbados and Jamaica today stems not from destiny but from the choices their leaders made in the face of two such events—the oil price shock of 1973 in the case of Jamaica and the oil price shock of 1990 in the case of Barbados.

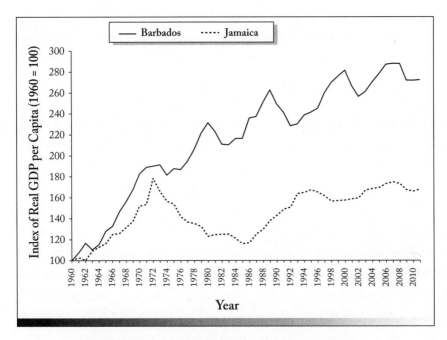

FIGURE 2.1: RICH ISLAND, POOR ISLAND:
STANDARDS OF LIVING IN BARBADOS AND JAMAICA
DIVERGE AFTER INDEPENDENCE

Any rise in the cost of fuel in a small country dependent on foreign energy has a cascading effect on the price of electricity, bus fare, and other basic goods and services. To make matters worse, higher fuel prices reduce economic activity, so that the increased cost of living dovetails with falling personal incomes. Higher inflation and lower growth are a dangerous duo for the leader of any country, let alone a leader in the developing world, where a majority of voters endure a daily struggle for survival. Faced with the adversity of an external shock to prices and incomes plus an angry electorate, what is a leader to do? Fundamentally, the choice boils down to this: implement policies that accommodate the desire to maintain previous spending patterns—a tactic that plays well at the polls but ultimately runs the country into a ditch—or adapt to the changed reality.

At pivotal moments, the government of Barbados made disciplined choices while Jamaica did not, and the consequences continue to have a staggering impact on standards of living in both places. From fiscal deficits and foreign trade to the money supply and the way governments treat labor and capital, policies matter, and there are big lessons to learn from the differences in the way the leaders of these small places conducted their economic affairs during the past four decades.

The Present Value of Populism

When Jamaica gained independence from Britain in 1962, the Jamaican Labor Party (JLP) held a parliamentary majority. For the next ten years the JLP remained in power and real GDP per capita grew at a rate of 5.8 percent per year. Most of the income gains came from two sources. A strong US economy in the 1960s created a robust export market for Jamaican bauxite, and rising incomes in North America boosted growth in Jamaican tourism.

But all was not well. Growth in the bauxite sector drove up costs throughout the economy, reducing the competitiveness of Jamaica's agricultural sector and precipitating an exodus of workers from the countryside to the cities. Because of strong unions, wages in the manufacturing and service sectors did not adjust downward to absorb the excess labor released from agriculture. Consequently, during its first decade of independence Jamaica experienced the odd combination of strong growth coupled with a rising unemployment rate—from 13 percent in 1962 to 23.2 percent in 1972.

Rising unemployment, income inequality, accusations of extreme favoritism toward its supporters, and attendant societal tensions over race, class, and crime proved too much for the JLP at the ballot box. On February 29, 1972, the People's National Party (PNP) rose to power under the leadership of Michael Manley and his promise of "democratic socialism." The PNP and Manley won 56 percent of the popular vote, thirty-seven of the fifty-three seats in Parliament, and a majority among every class of voters except small farmers. A man of extraordinary intellect, energy, and charm, Manley generated great expectations in the run-up to the general election of 1972. He persuaded "the urban poor, the Rastafarian community, the intelligentsia, organized labor, popular artistes, and the Church to join him in a crusade for social justice."[6]

As Manley campaigned to the driving reggae beat of Delroy Wilson's "Better Must Come," he also won the confidence and support of the Jamaican private sector. Sixty percent of businesspeople and high-income professionals who participated in the 1972 election cast their vote for the PNP.[7] The business community believed that this charismatic man could unify the country and lay the foundation for a more prosperous and stable society. The prospect of a more unified Jamaica—one with fewer labor strikes, more efficient governance, and the social peace that comes with greater class mobility and a more equal distribution of income—raised expectations for a future with reduced risk and increased profits for business. This newfound optimism caused a massive revaluation of corporate assets. Between June 1971 and January 1972, the Jamaica Stock Exchange Index rose by 25 percent in inflation-adjusted terms (see Figure 2.2). By the time Manley was firmly ensconced as prime minister in May 1972, the index stood at an all-time high, having increased by more than 40 percent in value over the course of the previous year.

Expectations for what the future would bring changed markedly as "Better Must Come" took substantive shape and it became clear exactly how Manley intended to deliver on his promise of social justice and self-reliance. Social justice programs such as income redistribution through government job creation, housing development schemes, and subsidies on basic food items required an increase in the volume of spending. Money had to come from somewhere, but the increased expense could not be supported by tax revenues from a private sector constrained by the new policy of self-reliance. In principle, the business community liked the idea of Jamaica as a self-reliant country

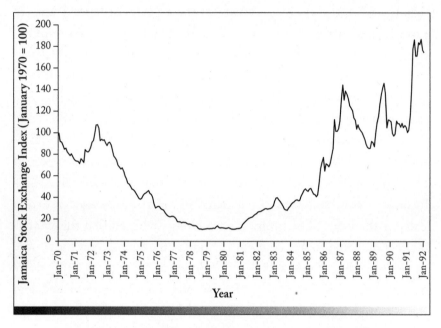

**FIGURE 2.2: THE JAMAICAN STOCK MARKET
COLLAPSED DURING MANLEY'S FIRST TWO TERMS
IN OFFICE**

with a diversified economy that was less dependent on bananas, bauxite, sugar, and tourism. But in practice, self-reliance translated as import substitution and government ownership of private enterprises. As the aspirations for a more unified and self-reliant Jamaica became manifest in a reality of policies that were, in fact, harmful for the business community, the previous sense of optimism evaporated. As the momentous election year drew to a close, the market was expressing a clear view that Manley's programs—however well intentioned—would ultimately destroy value rather than create it. By the time Manley gave his budget speech in May 1973, the stock market was already down 30 percent from its high a year earlier. Things only got worse from there as developments in the world economy clashed with Manley's goals.

In October 1973, the Arab members of the Organization of Petro-leum Exporting Countries (OPEC) initiated an embargo that tripled the price of oil and precipitated the global recession of 1974–1975. As tourist arrivals declined, the Jamaican economy suffered, but instead of reevaluating his priorities in light of a challenging external eco-nomic environment, Manley chose to double down on spending and adopted even more extreme policies. In the words of historian Arnold Bertram, "Nowhere do we get the impression that Michael Manley allowed himself to be fettered by the economic crisis of 1973."[8]

In its 1974 "Declaration of Principles," the PNP stated that the goal of domestic policy was "ultimate control by and in the name of the people of the major means of production, distribution, and ex-change."[9] And in pursuit of its aim to wrest the "commanding heights" of the economy—enterprises in strategic industries such as mining, energy, and transportation—from private control, the gov-ernment proceeded to buy banks, mines, hotels, utilities, and other businesses that many owners were all too happy to divest given the less-than-market-friendly environment. Because the government had no expertise in running the enterprises it bought, the process of nationalization simultaneously drained fiscal resources and under-mined national productivity. In the name of promoting self-reliance, the PNP erected import barriers, creating shortages of the goods that were needed for manufacturing, research, and other activities central to a modern economy. When foreign exchange reserves grew scarce, the PNP imposed exchange controls, but this only exacer-bated the problem by promoting capital flight as people moved their money offshore to escape restrictions. It was as if every time the economy sprung a leak the PNP stuck its finger in the hole, only to find that by doing so it created two more leaks that were worse still than the first.

It bears emphasizing that the PNP carried out all of its policies legally and within the framework of Jamaica's inherited institutions.

Manley's Jamaica of the 1970s was not Mugabe's Zimbabwe of today. There was no abrogation of the rule of law or detention of the opposition. Free and fair elections took place in December 1976. In spite of an imploding economy—GDP per capita fell by 8.1 percent in 1976—Manley managed to galvanize the support of the unemployed and working poor, with whom his social agenda remained popular, and won a second term. This time around only 20 percent of the business community voted for Manley—a stunning drop of support from the 60 percent figure in 1972.

Reasonable people may disagree about the merits of Manley's attempts to help the poor, but one fact about his economic and social agenda is beyond dispute: it was costly. Government spending rose from 23 percent of GDP in 1972 to 45 percent in 1978. Revenue did not keep pace with the rise in expenditure. From 1962 through 1972, Jamaica's average fiscal deficit was 2.3 percent of GDP. In contrast, from 1973 to 1980 the fiscal deficit averaged a whopping 15.5 percent of GDP. The PNP monetized much of the deficit by printing money, with predictable consequences. After averaging 4.4 percent per year from 1962 to 1972, inflation rose to 27 percent in 1980.

Manley's populist policies undermined both current prosperity and, as reflected in the forward-looking barometer of the stock market, the country's future well-being. With heightened risk and uncertainty, GDP in perennial decline, and no change of policy direction in sight, the Jamaican Stock Market Index declined in value during every year of Manley's first two terms, falling by an annual average of 24 percent. When Manley was voted out of office on October 30, 1980, the index sat at one-ninth of the level that had prevailed when he was first elected prime minister. Eight years of PNP policies destroyed almost 90 percent of the market value of Jamaica's publicly traded corporate sector. Ironically, the stock market, in some ways the ultimate symbol of wealth, had been signaling to Manley for eight years that his present policies would not only erode shareholder wealth but also steal the future hopes of the poor.

A rising market creates the virtuous circle described in the introduction to this book: higher stock prices reduce the cost of capital, thus driving up investment, employment, and wages. A plummeting stock market creates a vicious cycle that reverses this course. Consequently, as corporate valuations fell in Jamaica in the 1970s, so did investment (from 26 percent of GDP in 1972 to 14 percent in 1980), job creation, and employment prospects for the people Manley so desperately wanted to help. The 1980 unemployment rate in Jamaica was almost 30 percent. The fact is, government cannot uplift the masses by bashing business. To quote Bertram again, writing in the *Jamaica Gleaner*, "Manley's commitment to providing more for the poor in an economy producing less and less took its toll." Bertram's article ends with the observation that "a social revolution can only be sustained on the basis of a growing economy which offers opportunities for wealth creation on a level playing field."[10]

MANLEY, THE INTERNATIONAL MONETARY FUND, AND EDWARD SEAGA

During his first term as prime minister, Manley's stubborn commitment to his vision for the country blinded him to realities, but at the start of his second term, rising inflation, depleted foreign reserves, and massive unemployment forced the PNP to seek some measure of help from the International Monetary Fund. Manley had contentious dealings with the IMF on previous occasions, but in 1977 his government began a three-year stretch during which its relationship with the IMF went from bad to worse. Jamaica signed a loan agreement with the IMF in July 1977, only to have the IMF cancel it in December owing to Jamaica's noncompliance with the conditions. Talk of a new loan began again in January 1978, with the IMF continuing to insist that Manley adjust his policies to help Jamaica live within its means and implement reforms to raise productivity. But old habits die hard. Manley's inability to compromise eventually resulted in another failed agreement and a bitter parting of the ways with the IMF in March 1980.

General elections were set for the end of October, seven months after the break with the IMF. With the country's finances in shambles, the JLP made the economy a central issue of its campaign against Manley and the PNP. Led by Edward Seaga, a businessman and former university lecturer, the JLP captured fifty-one of sixty seats in Parliament.

The election of Seaga as prime minister marked a dramatic shift in Jamaica's economic policies. The JLP embraced a variety of economic reforms and moved quickly to end the tension that had escalated between Jamaica and the IMF during the 1970s. Specifically, in April 1981, Jamaica signed two loan agreements with the IMF totaling US$698 million.[11] In return, the JLP agreed to reduce the fiscal deficit and tighten monetary policy. Beyond short-term measures to stabilize the country's macroeconomic situation, the JLP also implemented a number of longer-term reforms under the auspices of a World Bank structural adjustment program. Seaga privatized state-owned enterprises (including some of those that Manley had nationalized), courted foreign direct investment, and generally moved to transfer factors of production from the public sector to private hands. In other words, although Secretary Baker had not yet made his famous speech and the term "Washington Consensus" had not yet been coined, when Seaga became prime minister in 1980, Jamaica began charting a new course that moved the country away from Manley's economic populism toward a set of policy reforms to restore growth.

The stock market expected these economic reforms to create value. During the six-month window from the 1980 election to the signing of the IMF agreements, the stock market rose by 45 percent (Figure 2.2). As the reforms continued, the Jamaican economy stabilized and the stock market steadily regained value, but it wasn't until August 1986 that the price of equity returned to its May 1972 level.

IT'S NOT PERSONAL

The stock market's differing reactions to the policies of Manley and Seaga were not personal. The market impartially assesses policies, responding positively to those that it expects to create economic value in the future and negatively to those that it anticipates will be destructive. The positive response of the Jamaican stock market to the economic policy announcements made soon after the PNP returned to power in February 1989 and Manley took office yet again underscores the market's focus on economic efficiency.

The PNP's platform this time around stood in dramatic contrast to its policies of the 1970s. The economic calamity of Manley's first two terms in office had been a Damascus Road experience. The extent of Manley's economic conversion comes through clearly in a 1990 post-election interview. Speaking about his first turn at the helm, Manley said:

> [The PNP], like many other people in the broad social democratic movement, placed greater reliance at that time on the capacity of the state to be a direct factor in production. Experience showed us that the state is not necessarily a reliable intervener in production. You stretch your managerial capacity and create tensions with the private sector that can be counterproductive. So the second great lesson that we learned is not really to depend on the government as a factor in production but rather to use government as an enabling factor for the private sector.[12]

Once back in power, Manley embarked on an economic liberalization and deregulation program that largely picked up where Seaga had left off. Manley and his party openly embraced a prominent role for private enterprise, free markets, and an economy more open to international flows of goods and capital. In November 1990, the PNP announced a new plan for privatization of some public services, and on June 28, 1991, Jamaica entered into a new $80 million agreement with the IMF. Health problems prevented Manley from seeing the PNP's economic reform agenda through to completion (he would die of prostate cancer on March 6, 1997), but by the time he retired on March 30, 1992, the stock market had risen 33 percent—a 250-percentage-point improvement over the market's 217 percent decline during his first turbulent tenure of the 1970s.

Although the stock market ratified Manley's shift in policy, going back to the IMF was a difficult pill to swallow, and many accused Manley of abandoning his principles. For example, in her book *Reclaiming Development*, Kari Levitt writes, "It is one thing to bow down to conditionalities imposed by international financial institutions. . . . It is quite another to adopt the ideology of the regime change introduced by Thatcher and Reagan."[13]

There is no question that the IMF demands that countries make difficult choices, but the experience of Barbados in the 1990s illustrates that even the smallest of nations can do so on its own terms if its leaders have the intellectual vision, moral courage, and negotiation skills to make their case.

BARGAINING IN
BRIDGETOWN

As war broke out in the Persian Gulf following the Iraqi invasion of Kuwait in the summer of 1990, the price of oil skyrocketed from an average of $17 per barrel in July to $36 in October. The oil price shock of 1990 delivered a one-two punch to the economy of Barbados. First, it hit costs, driving up the price of fuel, one of the country's major imports. Second, as the United States, the United Kingdom, and Canada tumbled into recession, the number of visitors from these nations to Barbados declined precipitously, striking a major blow to income. In 1990 the country's GDP per capita fell for the first time in seven years, contracting by 5.2 percent. The combination of a more expensive import bill and fewer tourist dollars with which to pay it led to a sharp increase in borrowing.

Against this backdrop, on January 22, 1991, the people of Barbados voted to keep the Democratic Labor Party (DLP) in power, trusting it to deal with the incipient crisis. The DLP's leader, Prime Minister Erskine Sandiford, began what would turn out to be a most eventful second term. A rocky road lay ahead for the fifty-four-year-old economist, but in retrospect the people of Barbados chose wisely.

Already in talks with the IMF about the possibility of a "stand-by arrangement"—the official term for the IMF's short-term (twelve to twenty-four months) loan that helps countries bridge temporary financing shortfalls—the government's first order of business was to stabilize the economy. The task fell most directly to Dr. DeLisle Worrell, an international economics expert at the Central Bank of Barbados, and a top-flight set of his colleagues from the Central Bank and the Ministry of Finance. Even as the team prepared a program to help Barbados adjust to its new circumstances, the economy continued to deteriorate, the fiscal deficit grew to 8.4 percent of GDP, and the country found itself on the brink of exhausting its foreign exchange reserves. A common rule of thumb is that a country should hold at least enough reserves to pay for three months' worth of imports. By the middle of 1991, Barbados could not cover the cost of *two weeks*. Time was of the essence.

A central point of contention in the government's discussions with the IMF had to do with the role of the exchange rate. Because much of what Barbados consumes it imports from abroad—items like cars, cereal, and televisions in addition to energy—the country's exchange rate has a major impact on inflation and the purchasing power of its people. When the Barbadian dollar loses value against the US dollar, American goods such as Corn Flakes become more expensive for Barbadian consumers. Maintaining a constant value of Barbados's currency against the US dollar provides a way for policymakers in

Barbados to fight inflation. Since 1975, the Central Bank had followed a fixed-exchange-rate policy, guaranteeing that anyone holding local currency could exchange their Barbadian dollars for US dollars at a rate of BDS$2.00 for US$1.00.

The downside to Barbados's policy is that a fixed exchange rate typically locks a country into a spiral of rising unit labor costs that makes its firms uncompetitive against rivals in countries whose exchange rates are allowed to lose value against the US dollar and other major currencies. This occurs because the prices of globally traded goods are determined by world economic conditions and set in US dollars, while wages are driven by domestic conditions and set in local currency. The combination of rising wages and a fixed exchange rate creates a loss of profitability for firms unless the productivity of their workers increases at least as rapidly. Short of a concerted national effort to raise productivity and/or restrain wage growth, this equilibrium seldom prevails. As of the 1990 economic downturn, Barbados was no exception to this rule.

The IMF argued that devaluing the Barbadian dollar—increasing by edict the number of Barbadian dollars it took to buy one US dollar—would revive the economy by making Barbados a lower-cost producer of traded goods and a less expensive destination for tourists. The weaker value of the Barbadian dollar would also make imports more expensive, but the IMF saw this as desirable: Barbadian consumers would buy fewer imported goods, and exporting more and importing less would stimulate production, return the economy to full employment, and increase the net inflow of foreign exchange so that the Central Bank would no longer have to worry about running out of reserves.

The preceding logic notwithstanding, the prime minister and his advisers resisted the IMF's recommendation to devalue. In addition to fearing the anger of a population that would have to pay more for Corn Flakes, they worried that devaluing the currency would set off a chain reaction of inflation-stoking events. Anticipating the higher cost of living that would result from devaluation, workers in both the public and private sectors would ask employers for compensating wage increases; as wages began to rise more quickly, employers would raise the prices of their goods, driving inflation higher still.

While Barbadian policymakers did not want to devalue their currency, the downturn in the world economy required that the country engage in some kind of belt-tightening if it was to reduce the fiscal deficit, avoid running out of foreign exchange, regain competitiveness, and return to growth. Accordingly, the Barbadian leadership tried to persuade IMF officials that a devaluation of the currency was not the only way to stabilize the country's financial situation. Because wages and salaries comprised almost half of all government expenditure in Barbados, cutting the pay of government workers would significantly reduce the fiscal deficit. Lower wages would also reduce the demand for imported goods and help reverse the drain on foreign exchange— if a government wants its people to eat less imported food, it can either make the food more expensive or give them less money with which to buy it. In effect, Dr. Worrell and his team at the Central Bank and the Ministry of Finance argued that cutting wages and salaries could produce the results that the IMF wanted to see without running the risk of triggering more inflation.

The rub, of course, was that nobody likes having their wages cut. That is why the IMF urges governments to change exchange-rate policy instead. Devaluing the currency is a back-door wage cut that does not require public consent. Going through the front door is much more transparent (and therefore harder), but that is precisely the course on which the Barbadian leadership chose to embark.

On the last day of July in 1991, Prime Minister Sandiford called an emergency meeting of representatives from Barbados's trade unions and the private sector. His message was clear: Barbados was in the throes of an unprecedented economic crisis, the government was in discussions with the IMF about how to avert disaster, and Sandiford needed the help of all three parties at the table—employers, the government, and unions. Sandiford told the group that the IMF proposed to provide Barbados with emergency funding, but in return wanted the country to adopt a number of economic reforms, including a devaluation of the currency, the introduction of a stabilization tax to raise revenue, and a reduction in government spending on a range of items from health care and education to various subsidies to the private sector. In lieu of devaluing the currency, the government's plan to trim the deficit and restore cost competiveness was an 8 percent wage cut for all government employees that would remain in effect for eighteen months, plus a 10 percent reduction in the overall size of the public sector.[14]

Everybody at the meeting wanted to avoid devaluation, but the union leaders strenuously objected to the idea of an 8 percent wage cut and massive layoffs in the public sector. Recognizing the need to speak with one voice, the various unions formed the Coalition of Trade Union and Staff Associations of Barbados and began developing an alternative plan. Under the leadership of Sir Leroy Trotman, general secretary of the Barbados Workers' Union, the Coalition adopted a formal stance that Barbados was under siege by the IMF and submitted a twenty-two-point program to the government laying out its initial offer to save jobs and explore options other than cutting wages. Discussions with the government fell apart in September when the government sidestepped Trotman and took its proposal directly to the public-sector workers. Presenting the proposal as a clear choice between a temporary wage cut and a devaluation with long-term consequences, government officials asked the workers to sign, on public record, a form indicating where they stood. Facing the Scylla of devaluation and the Charybdis of lower pay, a majority of them voted to accept the government's plan.

On October 1, 1991, Sandiford and the DLP slashed public-sector pay by 8 percent, fired more than 2,000 casual and temporary workers, introduced shorter workweeks, and adopted a series of other measures to reduce government expenses. Tempers flared. Appalled by the government's audacity, the Coalition coordinated two nationwide demonstrations. First on October 24, and then again on November 4–5, an estimated 30,000 protesters—the rough equivalent of 36 million Americans in front of the White House, or 6 million Britons converging on 10 Downing Street—marched through the streets of Bridgetown, calling for Sandiford's resignation. In addition to organizing protests, the Coalition challenged the wage cut in court, arguing that the government had negotiated in bad faith and violated the constitution.

The Barbadian stock market took note of the heightened state of uncertainty. Barbados first established a national stock exchange index, the BSE 100, on January 1, 1988. This date was too late to allow for a pair-wise comparison with Jamaica during the 1970s, but just in time to make it possible to examine the BSE 100's response to the adoption of stabilization measures in 1991. Following the protests, the BSE 100 lost value in four consecutive months and fell by another 3 percent in February 1992, when Barbados finally succeeded in convincing the IMF of the merits of the wage cut in lieu of devaluation and signed a $17 million stand-by arrangement. Did the stock market fall because people thought the government's program would hurt the economy? Or was the decline in share prices due to a heightened sense of risk—a fear that Barbadian society would come apart at the seams, undermining the government's ability to see the stabilization program through to completion? The sequence of events that transpired after the formalization of the IMF agreement suggests the latter.

Although Her Majesty's Privy Council ultimately upheld the government's right to cut wages, the reforms required a social compact in order to be sustained. A stool needs three legs to stand, and from October 1991 through the time of the IMF agreement, only the government and the unions participated meaningfully in the discussions. What ultimately got firms fully engaged was not their sympathy for the teachers and nurses who took pay cuts to save the country, but the realization that the private sector needed to share the pain of adjustment to ensure its own viability. Protests in the street were bad for business, and if the wage cut did not hold, the government would need to find money elsewhere. Owners of capital saw the writing on the wall and formed the Barbados Private Sector Association (BPSA) to represent their interests and participate more actively in the three-way discussions between business, the government, and the unions.

With the help of the Anglican Church, the government managed to reconvene the discussions, which had come to a halt in the aftermath of the marches on Bridgetown. In spite of tensions, the need for collective sacrifice prevailed as the leaders of each group took it upon themselves to help save Barbados. In a matter of months, and to his everlasting credit, Sir Leroy Trotman changed his position from mobilizing thousands in the streets of Bridgetown to humbly beseeching his members' support for the stabilization program.

In August 1993, the government, the unions, and the private sector signed a three-party protocol on prices and wages. The government kept its promise to not devalue the currency and paid back the IMF loan within eighteen months. Employers agreed to mitigate their price increases, accept lower profit margins, and open up their financial records to the unions; in return, private-sector workers assented to a wage cut of 8 percent and agreed to keep their demands for future pay raises in line with increases in productivity. All parties agreed to create a national productivity board to provide better data on which to base future negotiations.

What did the stock market think of the tripartite agreement? As it became clear that the country was on the verge of reaching a wage and price protocol, the market went on a tear. In March 1993, the BSE 100 rose by 4.7 percent. In April, it jumped by 8.7 percent, the largest monthly increase ever in the BSE up to that point in time. Overall, during the five-month window from the moment the public learned of the impending agreement and the date on which it was signed, the stock market rose by 20 percent in inflation-adjusted terms. Barbados's subsequent economic performance verified the market's judgment that the agreement was good news for the country's long-term economic prospects. The fall in wages restored external competitiveness and profitability, and the economy recovered quickly. From 1993 to 2000, GDP per capita in Barbados would grow by 2.7 percent per year, a sharp contrast to the contraction of 5.1 percent per year from 1989 to 1992.

Leadership's sustained commitment to the future paid great dividends for Barbadian society, but discipline sometimes carries a great personal cost. Just over a year after the signing of the tripartite agreement, the Barbados Labor Party defeated the Democratic Labor Party in the general election of 1994. The DLP did not return to power for fourteen years, and Sandiford, the man who guided Barbados through its worst economic crisis as a sovereign nation, would never again be prime minister. When asked by a journalist whether the sacrifice was worth it, Sandiford replied, "I think that the price that I paid was small in comparison to the good that came to the country."[15]

The response of Barbados's leadership to the crisis brought on by the 1990 oil price shock demonstrates that one size need not fit all when it comes to economic policy. The country's economic team rejected the IMF's tough medicine for restarting growth, but they did not pretend that Barbados could carry on with business as usual. The team considered alternatives and constructed a viable approach that was more palatable to the Barbadian people. The wage and price protocol achieved the same results as devaluation—reducing the deficit and restoring competitiveness—but avoided the risk of exacerbating inflation and, perhaps most importantly, forced a productive if contentious dialogue between government, workers, and employers about the future of their country. Although the process of communication was clumsy and input was solicited under duress, the people most affected by the reforms were ultimately consulted. Had Sandiford chosen the unilateral route of devaluation, a wage cut without consultation, his electoral outcome would have been the same, but the national dialogue about productivity, wages, and industrial relations—the fundamental long-run determinants of Barbados's prosperity—would not have happened.

Small Places, Big Ideas

Leaders have no control over the geographic location of their country, its colonial heritage, or the origins of its legal system, but they do have agency over the policies they implement. At critical moments in their post-independence histories, policymakers in Barbados and Jamaica picked very different paths, with staggering consequences for their countries' standards of living that persist even now. Yet a common thread worth emphasizing runs through the history of these two Caribbean nations: in each place, the stock market correctly predicted that sustained commitment to the future would improve the country's fortune and that failure to come to grips with reality would lead to economic ruin. Indeed, there are politically expedient ways to respond to the legitimate demands of an electorate and then there are disciplined approaches. Such a choice now sits squarely in front of leaders in the United States.

Incensed by their impression that banks and the top 1 percent of income earners received billions of dollars of bailout money from the US government during the financial crisis of 2008–2009, members of the protest movement "Occupy Wall Street" define themselves as champions for the 99 percent of the population who got nothing but the short end of the stick. Whatever you think of Occupy Wall Street, the outrage and frustration that ignited the movement is palpable and real. At the other end of the political spectrum, but arguably no less agitated, the Tea Party and its adherents air their utter discontent with the government's handling of the US economy. From Zuccotti Park to the Taxpayer March on Washington, angry Americans of different stripes now share the same rallying cry that mobilized the Jamaican masses in 1972: "Better must come!"

There are few secrets about the broad outlines of a helpful direction. For a start, the United States needs to reduce its long-term deficit to prevent the cost of servicing the national debt from reaching the point where it overwhelms our ability to make investments that increase productive capacity. The bipartisan National Commission on Fiscal Responsibility and Reform led by Erskine Bowles, chief of staff during the Clinton administration, and former Republican senator Alan Simpson has recommended a combination of spending cuts and tax increases as the most efficient way to reduce the deficit. By refusing to budge from their position of absolutely no tax increases during the acrimonious debate of the summer of 2011—when the United States came recklessly close to defaulting on its debt—lawmakers on the right made it clear that they were more interested in scoring political points with their base than in finding solutions.

The left is equally capable of political intransigence when it speaks of income inequality exclusively in terms of taxes. Tax rates on the top 1 percent of income earners may need to rise as part of the solution to the long-term deficit problem, but instituting higher tax rates on the wealthiest Americans is at best a small part of the solution to income inequality. A grossly inadequate educational system is the key issue. In a world where technological advancement inexorably continues to drive up the demand for high-skilled workers, the United States needs to make vast improvements in the education it delivers to a wide range of the population. Augmenting the supply of high-skilled workers over time will both increase the number of people in high-wage income brackets and mitigate the growth of the wage gap between high-skilled and lesser-skilled workers.

Education, not taxes, is the key to narrowing the distance between the haves and the have-nots in the United States, but macroeconomic policy can also have a profound impact on a society's capacity to accumulate skills. Policy decisions that increase efficiency expand the size of the pie and the quantity of resources at the disposal of the private and public sectors for investment in a range of national priorities. Moreover, almost any conversation about how to divide the pie becomes easier as the pie grows. By creating more resources to deal with questions of fairness, leaders can have an enormous impact on standards of living in less than a generation.

Moving past Washington, a range of developed-world capitals now find themselves confronting a choice between prudence and populism, between efficiency and fairness. In the aftermath of the Great Recession of 2008–2009, countries large and small face critical economic policy questions. Should Portugal, Ireland, Italy, Greece, and Spain stay the course and persist with the hard work of making their economies viable within the Euro Area by implementing the necessary economic reforms: fiscal discipline, freer flows of goods and capital, increased reliance on private enterprise, and more flexible labor markets?

Viewed through the lens of the stock market, the tectonic shifts in economic policy that have taken place in the developing world over the past few decades provide invaluable real-world lessons that the First World might use to address its present economic predicaments. Although the stock market has limited power to assess the likely impact of any single policy event (such as happened when the market misread Manley's true intentions in the run-up to the 1972 election), its average reaction to a large number of similar events in different countries over time is one of the most reliable predictors we have of the economic impact of changes in policy.[16] A more systematic analysis of stock market responses can now move us past the waters of the Caribbean and help with our efforts to resolve the broader global fight over economic reform.

CHAPTER 3

THE FIGHT REVISITED

LIFE IS FULL OF DIFFICULT DECISIONS THAT HAVE TO BE made on the basis of limited information. Even the simple act of selecting a restaurant for dinner commits you to a course of action with a likely price tag and an uncertain outcome. However, if you base your selection on the Zagat restaurant guide's aggregation of the opinions of thousands of previous customers, you can have some measure of confidence about what to expect from your upcoming dining experience. Deciding where to eat is a lower-stakes exercise than choosing a direction for economic policy, but leaders who want to make the right decisions for their countries can turn to an equivalent guidebook in the form of the stock market.

A statistical examination of the reactions of developing-country stock markets to the introduction of reforms in the mid-1980s delivers a robust set of facts on which we can base a useful, if preliminary, answer to a fundamental question that matters deeply for the lives of billions of people in both the developing and developed world: is it possible for policymakers to have a reasonable expectation, rooted in reality, that initiating an economic reform agenda will improve the future performance of their economy and create material value?

Critics of reform claim that major changes to developing countries' economic policies have not, in fact, delivered value. In support of their view, they often draw comparisons between East Asia and Latin America following the advent of reform in 1985. It is true that those who expected reforms to propel Latin America quickly to East Asian–style success were sorely disappointed. From 1985 to 2005, the East Asian economies grew by 7.4 percent per year, versus 2.9 percent in Latin America. But the relevant comparison is not Asia with Latin America, but rather Latin America with itself. Latin America's economic performance did improve substantially after it embarked on the path to reform, and shocking as it may seem, in comparison to expectations based on the economic record of the previous decade, Latin America actually outperformed Asia during the era of reform. Instead of arguing about whether critics or advocates of the Washington Consensus are correct, we can use the stock market to rise above the fight that America's former Treasury secretary, James Baker, started in 1985.

GREAT EXPECTATIONS

Long before Secretary Baker delivered his October 1985 speech in Seoul, word had spread that he intended to unveil a major new initiative to address the Third World Debt Crisis. During the months between the spring and fall of 1985, officials at the US Treasury and the Federal Reserve Board of Governors had an extended exchange of views about how to restore growth and lending to the developing countries. One former Treasury official described the genesis of the strategy as a set of ideas that Baker and Paul Volcker, then chairman of the Federal Reserve Board, formulated over a series of breakfast meetings.[1] When Volcker used the occasion of his May 13, 1985, remarks to the Bankers' Association for Foreign Trade in Boca Raton, Florida, as an opportunity to test-drive the concepts that he and Baker had been bandying about, the reality that a reform agenda was already in the works, as well as some of the specifics of what it might entail, became common knowledge in the world financial community.[2]

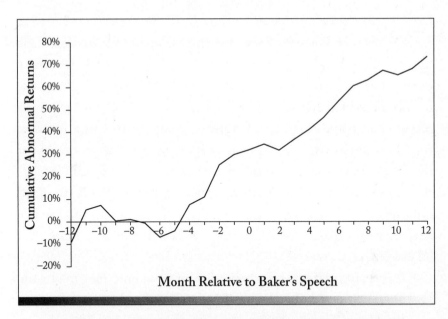

FIGURE 3.1: DEVELOPING-COUNTRY STOCK MARKETS
RESPONDED FAVORABLY TO THE BAKER PLAN

As news broke of the prospect of serious change, stock markets in developing countries immediately predicted that the new emphasis on reform would improve their economies. In the month after Volcker's remarks, the average stock market in countries targeted under the reform strategy experienced abnormal returns of 12 percent in real, local-currency terms (Figure 3.1). This is another way of saying that, after adjusting for inflation and performing econometric analysis that accounts for a wide range of other factors that might have driven up stock prices, total shareholder returns in these countries were, on average, 12 percent higher than they would have been in the absence of the news of impending reforms.

The set of ideas that evolved into the Baker Plan originally focused on fifteen countries, but the list later expanded to include seventeen in all.[3] Of those seventeen countries, reliable stock market data going back to 1985 exist for Argentina, Brazil, Chile, Colombia, Ecuador, Jamaica, Mexico, Nigeria, Peru, the Philippines, and Venezuela. Figure 3.1 illustrates the average behavior of the stock market in these eleven countries during the months before and after the official announcement of the Baker Plan. Instead of depicting market movements in calendar time, the picture is arranged according to event time to make it easier to infer the stock market's expectations about the future impact of the prospective shift in policy. For instance, between month "-5," when Volcker made his remarks in Florida, and month "0," when Baker finally gave his official speech, the average stock market experienced cumulative abnormal returns of more than 30 percent.

Baker would reiterate the centrality of economic reforms to the "US Proposal on the International Debt Crisis" in his testimony before the House Committee on Banking, Finance, and Urban Affairs two weeks after the Seoul speech. Lest there had been any doubt about the administration's commitment, between February 1986 and June 1987 President Reagan gave at least four sets of public remarks emphasizing his commitment to Baker's Plan.[4] As the extent of America's commitment to the reform agenda became more evident over the next several months, cumulative abnormal returns continued to rise, reaching 74 percent in the twelfth month after Baker's speech. Stated in US dollar terms, the cumulative abnormal returns in response to the Baker Plan produced a roughly $42 billion increase in market capitalization. The uniformity with which markets appreciated in value tells a story as important as the magnitude of the rise: the stock market in every one of the eleven countries experienced positive cumulative abnormal returns.

The multibillion-dollar revaluation of corporate assets and the uniformly positive response of multiple markets to news of the reforms reflected the great expectations bound up in the vision of economic reform that would come to be known as the Washington Consensus. The announcement of the Baker Plan sent an unmistakable message from the most important players in the world economic and financial system: if governments in developing countries wanted the financial support of the US government, the IMF, the World Bank, and international commercial banks, they had to stop searching for economic salvation in the school of dependency theory and embrace freer markets, fiscal temperance, and sound money. The private sector in developing countries thought that such changes would improve economic performance, anticipated that their governments were likely to adopt a subset of Baker's proposed reforms at some point down the road, and bid up stocks accordingly.

The anticipated shift in policy direction signaled by the Baker Plan was well received by the market—three cheers for business-friendly policies—but the news was also fraught with uncertainty. Would governments actually implement the reforms? How committed would they be? How long would it take to complete the reforms, and how long would it be until they began to have a positive impact on the economy? There are many potential obstacles to change, from leaders unwilling to accept the reality of resource constraints, to workers and corporations who (naturally) value their individual interests and might attempt to influence local officials through campaign contributions or less delicate means. These concerns and more were on the minds of rational market participants when news of the Baker Plan entered the public domain, and the uncertainty they caused surely tempered the stock market responses. Had the private sector in each developing country been certain of its government's willingness and ability to implement and sustain appropriate reforms, in all likelihood stock markets would have soared.

The stock markets' skepticism was certainly understandable. Failed attempts to reduce inflation and modernize the economies of Latin American countries were already a familiar part of that region's economic landscape by the time Baker unveiled his reform agenda. Indeed, given the late Paul Samuelson's famous quip—"The stock market has predicted nine of the last five recessions"—an important question is whether the optimism of developing-country equity markets was in any way justified by subsequent economic performance. Samuelson's observation that the market sometimes makes prediction errors warns us to complement stock market forecasts with data that measure whether economic performance actually improved following the onset of reform—a post-dining-experience assessment of the Zagat's guide, as it were.

THE POWER OF (INCREASING) PRODUCTIVITY

If we wanted to look at a single indicator of economic performance, productivity is a pretty good place to start. Productivity, also called "GDP per worker," measures the efficiency of a country's labor force. It is the total amount of goods and services produced in a country over the course of a year divided by the total number of workers—that is, the average output of goods and services produced by each worker. Productive countries are rich, unproductive countries are poor, and the only way for a country to sustainably increase its standard of living is to improve its productivity.

Data from the US economy give a sense of the extent to which productivity growth drives growth in GDP per capita. In the so-called golden age of growth between 1948 and 1973, the productivity of the US labor force grew by 2.8 percent per year and GDP per capita grew by 2.3 percent per year. From 1974 to 1982, US productivity growth fell to 0.8 percent per year and growth in GDP per capita also declined, to 1 percent per year.

So what of the Baker Plan countries? It is instructive to begin by focusing on a subset of six of the largest countries in Latin America: Argentina, Brazil, Chile, Colombia, Mexico, and Venezuela. Figure 3.2 reveals that in the ten years prior to the Baker Plan, productivity declined in all six countries, from a rate of −1.4 percent per year in Argentina to −3.8 percent per year in Venezuela. Not to put too fine a point on it, workers in these six Latin American countries became less

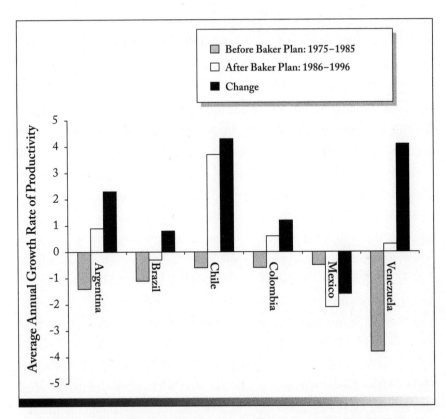

**FIGURE 3.2: PRODUCTIVITY GROWTH IN LATIN AMERICA
INCREASED AFTER THE ONSET OF REFORMS**

efficient for an entire decade: the levels of output per worker—and therefore standards of living—in the six Latin American countries were lower in 1985 than in 1975.

Although developing countries should have lower levels of productivity than rich countries such as the United States—that is, after all, what it means to be a developing country—we do not expect them to experience declining productivity. In fact, economic theory tells us that rates of growth in productivity in the developing world should, if anything, exceed those in developed countries, because there is so much scope for developing economies to catch up by importing ideas from abroad and adopting production techniques from rich countries instead of having to develop those techniques themselves. Why, then, did these six countries experience a decline in productivity from 1975 to 1985? A big part of the answer is inflation. And inflation plays a key role, both in the story of turnaround in Third World countries and in the current problems facing advanced nations, because no country can afford to let inflation make a comeback.

In many people's minds, inflation and Latin America are inseparable, but it was not always so. In 1970 the average rate of inflation for the six countries in Figure 3.2 was about 12 percent per year—higher than in the industrialized economies but not wildly out of line with the times. Remember, before Paul Volcker became chairman of the US Federal Reserve Board of Governors in 1979 and used the weapon of tight monetary policy to slay the beast of runaway price increases, the United States had flirted with double-digit inflation for much of the 1970s. Unlike the United States and other industrialized countries that stabilized inflation and then permanently reduced it to single-digit levels, Latin American nations, you will recall, printed money during the 1980s to cover the budget deficits they could not finance by borrowing abroad because of the debt crisis. The monetization of deficits fueled rising inflation, and in 1980 the inflation rate in our subset of six Latin American countries stood at 42 percent, more than triple its level in 1970. By 1985 inflation in these countries had spiraled to 170 percent per year, with both Argentina and Brazil well on their way to hyperinflation of 1000 percent per year and more.

Thinking about the burden that inflation imposes on individuals brings to mind people pushing wheelbarrows of cash to the grocery store to buy bread, but its cost to the larger economy sets in long before inflation hits epic levels. Economic research shows that when inflation reaches roughly 40 percent or more per year, productivity falls off a cliff.[5] (Note that economists classify inflation rates of 40 percent or more as high, 10 to 40 percent as moderate, and low inflation as anything less than 10 percent per year.) When prices increase that rapidly, the time and energy that workers spend worrying about the eroding value of their paychecks becomes a significant distraction as households become consumed with trips to the bank in an effort to cash in their wages before things get worse. The poor suffer most. In the words of a wicker vendor during Brazil's high-inflation era, "The rich can find ways to protect themselves, but inflation is doing to the poor . . . what the piranhas of the Amazon do to a cow in the water."[6]

On the business-management side, inflation forces entrepreneurs to divert their energy away from innovation and toward the stopgap measures of altering price structures. As employers, they become embroiled in a struggle to maintain viable relationships between labor costs and productivity.

Consider a company that makes a variety of products that comprise the typical basket of goods used by consumers. High inflation often causes the price of labor to rise more quickly than the price of the basket. When this happens, workers experience an increase in the "real wage," the wage (cost of labor) divided by the price of the basket. If this situation persists without a commensurate increase in productivity, the company will suffer shrinking profit margins, cut back on production and investment, and eventually lay people off. The point is not that an increase in real wages is bad, but that real wage increases driven by the dynamics of high inflation eventually undermine production and employment.

The real wage is an example of what economists call a "relative price," in this case, the price of labor relative to the price of goods. In efficient economies, relative prices fluctuate in accordance with changes in underlying fundamentals such as technology, tastes, and productivity. In contrast, the uncertainty created by high inflation causes relative prices to fluctuate in a harmful way.

High inflation also has harmful side effects on governments, which react by enacting policies that further undermine productivity, and a destructive, self-reinforcing spiral ensues. The interaction of inflation with fiscal policy provides one dramatic example of this phenomenon.

If taxes are paid this year on income received last year and this year's price level is twice as high as last year's, the real value of taxes collected is cut in half. As high inflation reduces government revenue, it increases the budget deficit and tempts the government to print more money, which in turn causes yet more inflation, and the economy heads down a dangerous path.[7]

Until inflation is under control, nothing else really matters—there is little time or latitude for leaders to contemplate medium-run issues such as whether to open the economy to free trade or sell off state-owned enterprises. With high inflation being so harmful to economic activity, Baker focused his speech on the need for policies to reduce it. In the decade following the Baker Plan, most countries succeeded in stabilizing and reducing inflation. It took a long time, and there were many fits and starts, but in the mid-1990s a marked downward trend began to emerge. By 1995 the average inflation rate in Latin America had fallen to 32 percent per year—still high compared to most countries around the world but significantly lower than the three- and four-digit figures of the previous ten years.

The fall in inflation raised economic efficiency. In the ten-year period from 1985 to 1995, every country except Mexico experienced an increase in its rate of productivity growth. The average productivity growth rate rose by 2.3 percentage points in Argentina, 0.8 percentage points in Brazil, 4.3 percentage points in Chile, 1.2 percentage points in Colombia, and 4.1 percentage points in Venezuela. The numbers on growth in GDP per capita (not shown in Figure 3.2) were similarly positive. For our six Latin American countries, the average growth rate of GDP per capita from 1975 to 1985 was 1.1 percent per year. From 1986 to 1996, the average growth rate of GDP per capita was 3.5 percent per year, an improvement of 2.4 percentage points.

The human significance of a 2.4-percentage-point increase in the growth rate of GDP per capita is not inconsequential. A country whose GDP per capita grows at 3.5 percent per year will double its standard of living once every twenty years. A country that grows at

1.1 percent a year will take sixty-four years to double its material well-being. This means that in a country that grows at 3.5 percent per year, the average person who lives to be seventy-five years old can expect her standard of living to rise more than eightfold over the course of her lifetime. Put that same person in a country that grows at 1.1 percent per year and her standard of living will barely double.

The consequences of the actions taken by developing-country officials in the two decades following the unveiling of Washington's economic reform agenda for the Third World eventually validated the markets' guarded optimism. Inflation receded, markets opened to trade, debt problems became less severe, governments regained access to international capital markets, and foreigners found the region a more welcoming place in which to invest. Critics will counter that for all of its reform efforts, Latin America did not achieve anything close to East Asian growth rates during the period. But again, the germane comparison is not of Latin America to Asia, but of postreform Latin America to itself before the onset of reform. Turning our attention from productivity measures back to stock market valuations throws into relief just how much Latin America's economic performance actually improved.

MANY HAPPY RETURNS

One of the best ways to understand the permanent economic impact of the steady accretion of policy changes over time is to shift our focus from the abnormal returns caused by the markets' initial reaction to the advent of reform to a measure called the "price-earnings (P/E) ratio," viewed over the entirety of the pre- and postreform epochs. A country's P/E ratio is the price of its stock market index divided by the market's total earnings over the previous twelve months. The great utility of the P/E ratio is that it functions like a unit price in a grocery store. Just as a unit price tells you the underlying cost per unit of the item irrespective of the total quantity that you purchase, the P/E ratio indicates how much you pay for each dollar of earnings when you buy a share of the country's stock market index. When a country's P/E ratio is low, stocks are cheap; when the P/E ratio is high, stocks are expensive to buy (and valuable to own).

As policy became less volatile, more disciplined, and more focused on enabling the private sector to operate efficiently, uncertainty declined and so did the rate at which shareholders discounted expected future earnings. The reduction in discount rates caused the average P/E ratio in Latin America to rise from a low of 3.5 before Baker's speech to a permanently higher level of about 14 by the mid-1990s. But in order for the P/E ratio to attain a new, permanently higher level at which shares would be four times more valuable, stock prices had to grow more rapidly than earnings, which in turn had started growing faster because of the more salubrious economic environment.

With two sets of forces simultaneously driving up stock prices—the transition to a higher, steady-state P/E ratio and accelerating earnings—people who held their savings in Latin American equities benefited enormously from the sea change in the policy environment. From 1985 to 2005, the average total shareholder return on Latin American stocks was 14.7 percent per year, 3.9 percent of which came from dividend payments and 10.8 percent from capital gains (pure stock price appreciation).[8] Workers also gained from the reduction in uncertainty. The rise in P/E ratios reduced firms' cost of capital, spurring investment, which then drove up productivity and wages.[9]

In fact, people who put their savings in Latin American stocks did far better than those in Asia. Over the same two decades—a period of time in which Asia's economy grew faster and had lower inflation than Latin America—the average total shareholder return in Asia was only 7.1 percent, a dividend yield of 1.9 percent per year and capital gains of 5.2 percent. How could this be? Conventional wisdom says that high growth equals high returns and slow growth equals low returns. In fact, much of the rationale for allocating savings to emerging-market stocks goes something like this: economic growth in the developing countries will exceed that of the developed world for many years to come; therefore, stock returns in emerging markets will also outstrip those of developed markets. How did the stock markets of a slow-growth and high-inflation region deliver returns twice as strong as those of the Asian Tiger economies? The answer may surprise you.

Relative to initial expectations, Latin America actually outperformed Asia from 1985 to 2005. At first blush, this assertion sounds, well, *loco,* but the key word is "relative." Coming into the 1980s, the Asian Tigers had already experienced two decades of rapid growth, were well on their way to achieving the status of newly industrialized countries, and had generated great expectations for their future. In contrast, the early 1980s saw Latin America fall headlong into the Third World Debt Crisis. Inflation was high, growth was low, and perhaps most importantly, growth rates in the region had begun to diverge substantially from those in Asia.

High future growth implies high returns only if the stock market has not already capitalized that growth into current prices. Because some East Asian countries, like South Korea, had undertaken substantial restructuring of their economies as early as the 1960s, their stock markets had already priced in high expected future growth. In line with their prior track record of success, the average P/E ratio in Asia was already high—18.3 as of 1986, to be exact.[10]

In contrast, when there is good news about the future that is not captured in current profits, prices jump relative to earnings and existing shareholders experience unexpected capital gains. This was the case in Latin America from the mid-1980s through the mid-1990s. Latin America's low P/E ratio prior to the onset of reform reflected the dismal outlook for the region and the reality that Latin America had yet to embark on its odyssey of change. The road to Ithaca is long, and Latin America's reform efforts were not uniformly successful by any measure, but the very attempt to move the region in the direction of market-friendly policies was a pleasant shock to the private sector given the low expectations at the time. Latin America's postreform improvement in growth did not close the gap in living standards with East Asia, but it was a vast improvement over the past and a boon to the markets.

SURPRISES IN STORE?

The counterintuitive lesson of reform and returns in Asia and Latin America contains important parallels to keep in mind as America and Europe struggle to regain their economic footing. In July 2007, the Dow Jones Industrial Average closed above 14,000 for the first time and went on to an all-time high in October of that same year. As of June 2012, the Dow sat about 10 percent below its historic peak and was off even more with adjustment for inflation over the course of the previous five years. With the potential breakup of the euro and the expectation of below-average growth for the next several years, there is no shortage of bad news for the financial markets of the industrialized world beyond the United States.

The good news for developed countries, however, is that the experience of Latin America tells us that low-growth countries need not be low-return countries. Future growth in the emerging world may significantly outstrip GDP gains in advanced economies, but that does not mean that First World stocks will underperform. Owing to the heightened sense of uncertainty, P/E ratios in some developed countries currently sit below their historical averages. In the same way that Latin American stock markets transitioned back to their steady-state P/E ratios and delivered stronger total shareholder returns than Asia from 1985 to 2005—the period when uncertainty about reforms was being resolved—and just as GDP growth in Latin America over that same period beat initial expectations, developed-country stocks could outpace Asian markets over the course of the next decade.

First World policymakers could surprise both voters and the market by applying a few relevant elements of the reform agenda at home. The US Congress could pass bipartisan legislation to rein in the country's deficit and debt problems. Across the Atlantic, troubled European countries might seriously embrace structural reforms to raise productivity and improve competitiveness, even as their creditors agree to write down substantial amounts of their outstanding debt.

And make no mistake. Emerging markets—especially in Latin America, Africa, and the Middle East—also have a lot of work to do if they are to reach their full potential and serve as the even more powerful engine of growth the world economy needs to initiate and sustain a full-fledged turnaround. In many developing nations, reforms did not begin to take hold with anything approaching a sense of permanency until the mid-1990s, underscoring the protracted nature of the process.

Will the work that needs to happen actually get done? Part of the answer lies in the political economy of domestic reform, but it is also wrapped up in international relations. No country will thrive in a vacuum. It takes global coordination to sustain commitment to the future. We can have wise leaders—including those who use historical data as a guide to choosing a disciplined direction for economic policy—but in an interdependent world things can still go awry in the absence of cross-country cooperation. It's time to take a closer look at the connections between the powerful catch-up economics that transformed the Third World into modern-day "emerging markets" and the troubled set of international relations that threaten to undermine the process.

CHAPTER 4

PATHS (AND OBSTACLES)
TO PROSPERITY

EMERGING ECONOMIES PRODUCE ALMOST HALF OF THE
world's goods and services, and in 2009 they were the sole contribu-
tors to global growth, expanding by 2.4 percent while developed
countries contracted at an average rate of 3.2 percent.[1] Although predictions of the demise of advanced capitalist nations inevitably occur
whenever we hit a trough, the most recent economic downturn actually did differ from those of the past in an important way: unlike the
typical post–World War II recessions engineered by central banks in
an attempt to stem the rise of inflation, the proximate cause of the
Great Recession of 2008–2009 was the financial crisis that started in
the United States and spread to Europe.

History tells us that economies that tumble into recession because of
financial crises take longer to recover than those bouncing back from
garden-variety recessions.[2] Because the driving force behind this most
recent downturn differed substantially from the causes of previous economic contractions, the recovery will also take a different path. The financial crisis and the resulting mountain of First World debt make it
unlikely that the United States, Europe, and Japan will lead the recovery of the world economy, as these countries have done in the past. For
the first time in history, economic growth in emerging economies will

be the key to the growth of incomes and employment in the advanced economies, not the other way around.

The centrality of developing countries to the health of the world economy is readily apparent from their contribution to the income statements of Fortune 500 companies, ranging from the consumer packaged-goods industry to producers of capital goods. Coca-Cola, Procter & Gamble (P&G), and Caterpillar all depend on emerging markets for more than one-third of their total revenue.[3] P&G expects to add an additional one billion consumers in the coming decade, the vast majority of whom will come from emerging economies.[4]

Indeed, with the rise of production and consumption in the developing world, the road to renewed global prosperity runs less through New York, London, and Tokyo than it does through Shanghai, Mumbai, and São Paulo. Will the journey be bumpy or smooth? The answer turns fundamentally on which path governments of emerging countries choose to take, and it is far from clear which way they will go. Economist Andrei Shleifer refers to the past three decades as the "Age of Milton Friedman," a time when markets triumphed and lifted millions of people out of poverty.[5] Yet in spite of the market's demonstrated power to improve the human condition, and in light of the Great Recession, developing countries are at best skeptical market converts, and the potential for apostasy could not be more real. From the Argentinean government's recent expropriation of the oil and gas company Yacimientos Petrolíferos Fiscales (YPF) to protests in India, there are many signs of backlash against the economic reform agenda and the Western hegemony that brought it to the shores of the developing world.

In the realm of international economic relations, as in many other aspects of life, the tone of the messenger matters as much as the content of the message. Because advanced nations pushed reform in the 1980s and 1990s and then failed to acknowledge the progress of their colleagues in the developing world, the mantra of "stabilization, liberalization, and privatization" rings hollow to many among both the electorate and the elected in emerging economies. Since the world's return to rapid, sustainable, and inclusive growth hinges on more, not less, commitment by emerging economies to country-appropriate aspects of the reform agenda, the prospect of a future of shared prosperity now stands in jeopardy. To understand how to move forward in a constructive direction from this critical crossroads, we need to pull back the curtains on the process of reform and examine the connections between policy changes, economic growth, and the need for mutual respect between nations.

China provides a good place to start. Its economic transformation epitomizes "catch-up economics"—the process through which poor countries, by making disciplined policy choices, can grow faster than rich countries for an extended period of time, thereby closing the income gap between themselves and places like the United States, Japan, and Switzerland. There are many variations of catch-up, but in the end they all boil down to a fundamental truth: if a country wants to grow faster, it must increase the rate at which it accumulates capital, labor, and ideas and/or increase the efficiency with which it uses those factors of production. At its core, economic reform is not about ideology but the rather practical matter of triggering and sustaining catch-up by making policy changes that incentivize people to save, invest in physical and human capital, innovate, and employ workers where they are most productive. The story of China's gradual reforms illustrates the value of pragmatism at work.

CATCH ME IF YOU CAN: CHINA'S RISE IN THE WORLD ECONOMY

When Mao Zedong died in 1976, after thirty-one years as chairman of the Central Committee of the Communist Party of China, the country's economy was one-tenth of its current size, the term "emerging markets" had not yet been coined, and the phrase "Third World" was still a politically acceptable way to refer to the developing countries that then accounted for less than 20 percent of the world's output. It was also a time when the Cold War occupied center stage, dependency theory was in vogue, and newly independent countries throughout Africa, the Caribbean, and Latin America were attempting to grow through the use of policies such as import substitution and inflationary finance. The countries of East Asia, however, provided one exception to this trend. By the mid-1970s, South Korea, Singapore, Taiwan, and Hong Kong had already begun their unprecedented ascent out of poverty by stabilizing their macroeconomic environments and increasing trade with the rest of the world. Singapore, for example, abandoned import substitution and embraced an export-oriented growth strategy as early as 1965. That is to say, almost two decades before Washington unveiled its economic plan for the Third World, the countries that eventually would be dubbed the "East Asian Tigers" had already begun dabbling in economic reform.[6]

The rapidly increasing economic fortune of China's neighbors was not lost on Deng Xiaoping when he ascended to power in December 1978, a little more than two years after Chairman Mao's death. Unwilling to repeat the policy mistakes of Mao, under whom China experienced the death of millions from starvation, Deng adopted a "do what works" approach to the economy, shopping around for ideas that would improve living standards, regardless of their source or ideological bent. Deng's willingness to borrow relevant approaches from other nations evolved alongside China's new "open-door policy"—a commitment to opening up the country to free trade, investment, and the exchange of ideas. Having heard of Singapore's success, he visited the country to seek the advice of Prime Minister Lee Kuan Yew. He even consulted Western institutions such as the World Bank. Upon receiving the Bank's president, Robert McNamara, in 1980 during the organization's first official mission to China, Deng remarked, "We are very poor. We have lost touch with the world. We need the World Bank to catch up. We can do it without you, but we can do it quicker and better with you."[7]

A doggedly pragmatic man, Deng understood economic logic and had no objection to harnessing the power of the market, so long as it helped him achieve the Communist Party's goal of creating a wealthy and powerful China. Under his leadership, China embarked on a journey that threaded a careful path between economic reform, on the one hand, and maintenance of political control, on the other—a system that Deng termed "Socialism with Chinese characteristics." Deng's agenda centered on the "Four Modernizations": agriculture, industry, national defense, and science and technology. The Party began its economic transformation with agricultural reform.

Before Deng and under Mao, farmers were forced to join communes—rural administrative units responsible for a variety of economic and civic functions. Under this system of farm collectives, each of which consisted of a large number of households, people shared everything. What were once individual assets—land, labor, and capital—became group property, and the commune leadership directed and managed the use of all resources. Because these agrarian households could not keep any part of their harvest for personal consumption or to sell for profit, individuals had little incentive to exert effort beyond a minimal level—a fact that became a matter of life and death for one part of China around the time of Deng's rise to power.

In 1978 an epic drought hit the province of Anhui, and starvation became widespread. The land reportedly became so dry that only the greatest individual exertion would render it arable.[8] But local farmers refused to put forth this kind of effort without the prospect of some personal benefit. In an act of desperation, the leaders of a small village called Xiaogang abandoned the communal farming system. They divided the land into private plots and gave farmers the right to keep or sell some of the proceeds of their labor. Given prior experiences during the Cultural Revolution, families swore a secret oath to raise each other's children if they were arrested for their participation in this new scheme.

Their bravery paid off. While the illegal arrangement was eventually discovered and generated a contentious exchange between provincial and national Party officials, Beijing ultimately assented because the experiment had a large positive impact on agricultural output. In fact, the Party extended the program to the entire country by repealing the system of communes and collectives and authorizing the Household Responsibility System (HRS).

The performance of Chinese agriculture improved dramatically after implementation of the HRS. Under communes and collectivization, China's agricultural productivity was no higher than it had been in medieval times, and the inefficiency of the system subjected the country to intermittent risk of food shortages, sometimes catastrophic.[9] The "Great Leap Forward," Mao's failed attempt at rural industrialization via moral exhortation instead of incentives, resulted in the deaths of tens of millions of people. In contrast, from 1978 to 1984 the real income of farm households increased by 60 percent, and over the next two decades agricultural productivity rose tenfold.

The potential to profit from their own work proved a powerful incentive for farmers. The share of agricultural output sold in open markets rose from 8 percent in 1978 to 80 percent in 1990, triggering the rise of entrepreneurship and manufacturing in two unanticipated ways. First, the open market in agricultural products created jobs in trading, transportation, storage, construction, and other complementary services. Second, as the supply and variety of food available to urban dwellers increased, they joined with farmers in support of the reform process, creating momentum for further experimentation.

As an integral part of the reform process, China promoted the growth of manufacturing by legalizing the creation of privately owned firms. During the late 1980s, the Party under Deng decentralized much of its economic planning to the provincial level, allowing the rise of community-owned businesses that offered both employment for locals and creative goods and services. Additionally, the Party established a system that incentivized greater risk-taking in state-owned enterprises (SOEs) by rewarding them based on their performance and allowing them to retain net profits.

China also harnessed the power of foreign direct investment as an engine of manufacturing growth. Western firms began flocking to China to take advantage of low wage rates, close proximity to fast-growing markets, and the government's newly created economic zones. For example, in export-processing zones such as Shenzhen, Guangdong, and Fujian, firms were allowed to import raw materials duty-free as long as they used those materials to manufacture goods for export. On February 1, 1980, the country's export sector received a boost as China regained its "most favored nation" status with the United States—a beneficial trade designation that President Harry Truman had stripped from all Sino-Soviet bloc countries in 1951. In tandem with this change, China began slashing its tariff rates and pursuing mutually beneficial trade relationships with the United States and other Western nations.[10] In December 2001, China formally joined the World Trade Organization (WTO), and its membership brought the benefits of reduced tariffs on Chinese products to markets across the world, along with improved availability and quality of foreign goods and services to Chinese consumers.

As factories went up and enterprises became more efficient, China turned into the world's chief producer of toys, garments, and other manufactured goods. Workers who were no longer needed for the planting and cultivation of inland fields moved to coastal provinces to work in the manufacturing sector. With millions of workers moving from fields to factories, wages stayed low in spite of the soaring demand for labor. As a result, manufacturing remained profitable and a virtuous cycle ensued. Investment boomed, employment grew, GDP expanded, and incomes rose. The World Bank estimates that the Chinese economy lifted more than half a billion people out of poverty between 1980 and 2007.

In the framework of catch-up economics, China attained record rates of economic expansion because it managed to increase the growth rate of all three factors of production. It brought enormous quantities of people out of inactivity and underemployment in rural areas into gainful and more productive employment in the cities. China also promoted rapid rates of capital accumulation by permitting entrepreneurs to start their own businesses and keep the profits. Yet as important as capital and labor are for catch-up growth, ideas are the most vital input. Ideas range from new technologies—tractors instead of hoes, drip irrigation instead of buckets—to policies that provide incentives to employ both capital and labor more productively. By improving the productivity of existing resources, better ideas cause a country's output of goods and services to expand even if its stock of capital and labor do not. The Chinese government increased the growth rate of ideas by "importing" policies that substituted many elements of a market economy for the elements of state planning. As investment became more profitable, foreign firms entered China, bringing with them still more new ideas—not about policy, but about things like supply chains, marketing, distribution, and sales.

From
Tortoises to Hares

The forces of catch-up economics, far from being confined within the borders of China, have been at work in the broader developing world for some time and continue to shift the center of economic gravity toward emerging economies. In addition to their disproportionately large impact on global growth, emerging economies now consume more than half of the world's energy, hold the majority of the planet's foreign exchange reserves, and account for almost 50 percent of exports.[11] Moreover, as incomes continue to rise in emerging-market countries, their citizens will buy more goods from the rich world. This is one of the reasons why strong growth in emerging economies is central to economic recovery in the developed countries. But the most striking observation about emerging markets is not where they are now but what they may yet become if the process of catch-up continues unabated over the next few decades—or if it stalls.

In 2001 economist Jim O'Neil of Goldman Sachs coined the term "BRICs" as an acronym for the four large and increasingly important emerging economies of Brazil, Russia, India, and China. Two years later, Dominic Wilson and Roopa Purushothaman of the Goldman Sachs economics research team used the principles of catch-up economics to produce an astonishing report about the future prospects of the BRIC countries.[12] The report projected that by 2025 the BRICs could easily be one half the size of the world's six largest economies combined (the United States, Japan, the United Kingdom, Germany, France, and Italy)—a remarkable conclusion considering that they are currently less than 15 percent as large. Furthermore, Mexico, South Africa, Turkey, Vietnam, and other large emerging economies are all viable contenders for BRIC-like status in the near future.[13] Wilson and Purushothaman predicted that by 2050 the world's six largest economies might include only two that are in that group today: the United States and Japan. Once the slow-growing tortoises of the global economy, emerging nations have now become the hares. But the question for hares, of course, is whether they can maintain the pace.

Based on sound analysis, the Goldman Sachs projections are neither fanciful nor controversial, but they rest on assumptions that, while reasonable, cannot be taken for granted. Specifically, the report assumes that the implementation of ideas—economic policy reforms such as stabilization, trade liberalization, and privatization—drove much of the economic catch-up by developing countries over the past three decades, and that the governments of emerging economies will continue to pursue economic reform agendas. Suspend disbelief about the former premise for the moment, as we will scrutinize its validity in subsequent chapters. What about the validity of the latter? Even if economic policy reforms do enable catch-up growth, is it clear that governments in the developing world will continue to implement them? A cursory examination of current events suggests that many leaders remain reluctant at best to make disciplined choices and expend the political capital needed to stay the course.

For example, after severing its ties with the IMF in 2003, the Argentinean government can now spend without the Fund leaning over its shoulder and whispering impolite words such as "budget constraints" and "inflation" in its ear. President Christina Fernández de Kirchner took full advantage of this freedom during the run-up to her reelection in October 2011. In response to reports of consumer prices rising at the rate of almost 25 percent per year, the Kirchner administration chose to deliberately underreport inflation and sacked the governor of the central bank because he refused to monetize the government's spending. This populist stance extends beyond willful disregard of rising inflation. In April 2012, the government began turning back the clock on privatization by expropriating a controlling share of Yacimientos Petrolíferos Fiscales (YPF), an oil and gas company that had been privatized in 1992 and is currently owned by the Spanish energy conglomerate Repsol. Part of a broader attempt by President Kirchner to tap into a rising tide of antireform sentiment, the renationalization of YPF threatens to strain relations with Spain, one of Argentina's most important trading partners. A robust Brazilian economy next door and strong global demand for grains such as soybean and corn continue to fuel the performance of Argentina's economy in the short run, but without tackling inflation, reining in public spending, and ending arbitrary taxation, it is not clear how long the good times will last. We have seen this story play out in Argentina many times before, and it has yet to end well.

Those governments that do try to follow the disciplined path continue to meet with forceful protests from their electorates. Consider the case of India, a country that, thanks to the business-friendly policy changes initiated under Rajiv Gandhi in the 1980s and deepened by the economic reform program of 1991, more than doubled its growth rate of GDP per capita—from 1.7 percent per year between 1950 and 1980 to 3.8 percent from 1980 to 2000. In this rapidly growing country that is now a world leader in call centers, information technology, and business process outsourcing, the efforts of Prime Minister Mahoman Singh (chief architect of the 1991 program) to reduce fuel subsidies and open the country's retail market to foreign companies met with fierce resistance in September 2012. A national strike protesting the government's reform agenda caused an estimated $2.3 billion of lost industrial production, and in the states of Bihar and Uttar Pradesh protesters blocked railroad tracks and burned an effigy of Prime Minister Singh.[14] Whether it is governments flouting received wisdom or citizens protesting major policy decisions, much of the developing world's antipathy toward the economic reform agenda flows from the history of its relationship with the purveyors of economic advice.

RESISTANCE AND RESENTMENT

Effective communication and mutual respect are as vital to good relations between countries as they are to a happy marriage. Today, owing to poor communication and unreciprocated respect, the economic union between developing countries and the developed world is on thin ice. Specifically, the economic policy changes adopted by emerging markets over the past three decades—policy changes that arguably provide the key to their catch-up success—stand in danger of rejection, for three reasons.

First, America and Europe repeatedly fail to practice the reform agenda that they preach and promote through international economic institutions like the IMF, the World Bank, and the World Trade Organization. Second, people perceive the IMF as indiscriminately prescribing the same set of policy changes to all countries that approach it for money, irrespective of their individual circumstances. Third, the power-sharing arrangements of the IMF and the World Bank fail to acknowledge the catch-up success that developing countries achieved by putting in place the very policy changes they recommended in the first place. Many developing countries did what was asked of them but still find their voices ignored around the tables at which decisions get made about the world economy.

The power of the WTO, the World Bank, and the IMF stems from the circumstances of their creation. In 1944 world financial leaders gathered in Bretton Woods, New Hampshire, to build a set of institutions that would restructure the world's trade and financial system, promote prosperity, and prevent the return of the protectionist policies that had contributed to the outbreak of World War II. The discussions about how to promote cooperation on international trade eventually resulted in the 1947 General Agreement on Tariffs and Trade (GATT)—the predecessor of today's World Trade Organization. Similarly, the decision to create the World Bank grew out of deliberations related to the long-run tasks of financing postwar reconstruction in Europe and economic development in poor countries. As for the IMF, it was created in 1945 to bear responsibility for the financial and monetary side of international economic cooperation—that is, to promote macroeconomic and exchange-rate stability and provide short-term financing to countries experiencing difficulty meeting their cross-border payment obligations.

Today the IMF plays a lead role in the global economy, providing surveillance of the economies of all 188 member countries, giving policy advice, and pulling nations back from the abyss when they get hit by financial crises. The IMF's short-term emergency loans enable countries to avoid default and maintain the flow of commerce when the private capital market grows skittish about their financial health and stops lending. In other words, like the US government's role as the "lender of last resort" for companies too big to fail, the IMF bails out countries. And like the US government's choice to bail out AIG and not Lehman Brothers, the IMF chooses the nations to which it will lend—and under what conditions.

Conditionality, or the lending of money to countries if and only if they agree to make specific economic policy changes, gives the IMF and its leadership considerable leverage over nations in precarious economic waters. The World Bank wields similar influence over its clients. Although the Bank's mandate is to channel funds to developing countries for long-term development, as opposed to the short-run crisis management undertaken by the IMF, the Bank also imposes conditionality, requiring countries to make structural adjustments in exchange for loans.

The strictures of conditionality are a bitter pill for any country to swallow. As in the case of Barbados, the IMF typically insists that governments reduce their spending, increase their revenue, and devalue their currency, which can increase unemployment and reduce living standards in the short term. World Bank structural adjustment loan conditions require changes that might range from reducing tariffs that protect domestic industries from foreign competition to removing regulations that restrict the ease with which employers can hire and fire workers. All of these measures, whether they are requested by the IMF or the World Bank, impose short-run costs and are an especially hard sell in developing nations because the highest level of IMF and World Bank leadership—the handful of individuals who ultimately set the terms of loan agreements—has always been dominated by developed countries. At the time when these two institutions were created, the Americans and Europeans had the power to select the leaders of the World Bank and the IMF, respectively. The ability of the Americans and Europeans to have their way reflected their disproportionately large contribution to the world economy at the time. Decades later, the composition of the world economy is dramatically different, but the process for choosing the leadership of the World Bank and the IMF is not.

For example, following the departure of Dominique Strauss Kahn as managing director of the IMF in the spring of 2011, emerging economies lobbied for an open, meritocratic selection process to find his successor. Europeans argued that the Euro Area debt problems at center stage in the world economy required a uniquely European perspective. Nobody had advanced such an argument for a Latin American or African national to head the IMF during the 1980s Third World Debt Crisis.

As for progress at the World Bank, when Robert Zoellick stepped down as president in the spring of 2012, many people—including thirty-nine former World Bank officials—believed that Nigerian finance minister Ngozi Okonjo-Iweala was the most qualified candidate for the job.[15] Instead, US president Barack Obama nominated an American, Dartmouth College president Jim Kim, making Kim's ascent to the top post a fait accompli. Reasonable people can disagree about any single choice between stellar candidates for an important leadership role, but the fact remains that for almost seventy years developing countries have accepted conditional loans from institutions that they have never had the opportunity to lead.

Although emerging markets do have representation on the executive boards of the Bank and the Fund, their voting shares are small in comparison with their importance to the world economy. The roughly 40 percent share of the votes they have on each of the executive boards is about ten percentage points less than their share of output in the world economy.[16] It is not difficult to see how this state of affairs might sow seeds of discord in the developing world. In the words of Trevor Manuel, South Africa's minister of finance from 1996 to 2009, "The old order has to pass."[17]

Underrepresentation in the voting structure is not the only source of strain in the relationship between developing countries and the international financial institutions. Critics deridingly joke that the letters IMF stand for "It's Mostly Fiscal." The Fund's typical (and often accurate) refrain to countries in crisis—that they need to cut their spending and/or increase revenue to repay their debts and lay a foundation for sustainable growth—is not well received because the messenger comes across as hypocritical in demanding things from developing countries that it does not require of advanced economies. For example, the IMF insisted that the governments of Korea, Indonesia, Thailand, and Malaysia reduce their spending during the 1997 Asian Financial Crisis. In contrast, when financial crisis struck the United States and Europe in 2008, the IMF actually recommended that the governments of the major developed countries *increase* spending.[18] The point here is not so much about substance (there were good reasons to implement a coordinated fiscal stimulus during the 2008 crisis) as it is about the perception of a double standard—that there are strict fiscal rules for the developing countries and only discretionary guidelines for advanced economies.

Angered by what they perceived as an inappropriate and harmful insistence on fiscal austerity by the IMF during the Asian Financial Crisis, and motivated by a desire to avoid a repeat experience with the Fund in the future, a number of Asian countries conceived the "Chiang Mai Initiative." Started in 2000 by the members of the Association of Southeast Asian Nations (ASEAN) plus China, Japan, and South Korea, the Chiang Mai Fund made $120 billion available to member countries and, more importantly, represented an Asian attempt to provide a regional alternative to the existing international arrangements for borrowing during times of crisis. Latin Americans adopted a similar tack when in 2006 they launched a proposal for Banco del Sur, a regional lender with $20 billion available to its members—Argentina, Brazil, Paraguay, Uruguay, Ecuador, Bolivia, and Venezuela. These attempts by emerging economies to increase their financial independence have real implications. Instead of relying on the IMF for crisis insurance, developing countries have sharply increased their savings and accumulation of foreign exchange reserves. IMF lending fell so dramatically in the decade following the Asian Financial Crisis that many observers wondered whether the institution would go out of business.

Recognizing that increasing disengagement by the fastest-growing economies in the world called their very raison d'être into question, the IMF, the World Bank, and the WTO mounted, with varying degrees of success, a number of efforts to repair their damaged relations with developing countries. On the superficial end of the spectrum, the IMF and the World Bank made changes to their voting structures in the spring of 2008 intending to give large emerging markets greater voice and power, but the new structures continue to deny emerging economies a voting share commensurate with their contributions to the world economy. For example, Brazil, Russia, India, China, and South Africa account for approximately 21 percent of world GDP and only 11.5 percent of IMF votes. In contrast, the European Union produces roughly 24 percent of global GDP but carries an outsized 32 percent voting share.

The IMF did institute substantive reform to its lending policies in the fall of 2008. In an attempt to address the criticism that it prescribes the same fiscal medicine for all countries irrespective of their individual circumstances, the Fund introduced a new lending instrument called the flexible credit line (FCL). Unlike typical IMF loans, the FCL offers uncapped access to funds with long payback horizons and minimal conditions to countries with a sustained track record of strong economic management. In spite of the IMF's best efforts, no country availed itself of the FCL during or after the darkest days of the 2008–2009 financial crisis.[19] This fact speaks volumes about the depth of the IMF's relationship problem with developing countries. It is difficult to be a lender of last resort and provide counsel for the world's fastest-growing economies if countries are reluctant to take your money or listen to your advice.

The WTO's ability and willingness to bring about substantive change for developing countries has also been less than stellar. The WTO operates in "rounds," which conclude when negotiations result in an agreement. The current set of negotiations, known as the Doha

Development Round, began in 2001 with the intention of, among other things, leveling the playing field in international trade for developing countries by reducing the barriers they face to selling their agricultural products to rich countries. Trade in agriculture is central to developing countries because a much larger fraction of their populations lives in rural areas. The prospects of a successful conclusion to the Doha Development Round appear vanishingly small after the spectacular collapse of negotiations in Geneva during the summer of 2008. Disagreement over trade in agricultural products remains one of the central sticking points. The Americans and Europeans insist on maintaining subsidies for their domestic farmers that effectively act as barriers to imports from the developing world.

Token attempts at democratization by the IMF and the World Bank, in combination with the inability of the WTO to deliver greater access to the benefits of free trade, make it easy to understand why developing countries have begun turning away from their strained relationships with these organizations. From the perspective of many emerging economies, increased self-reliance and an ability to form their own institutions underscore the power of catch-up economics.

But the ultimate goal is prosperity, not self-reliance. What if the rise of emerging markets is actually the consequence, to some extent, of their adoption of a subset of IMF, World Bank, and WTO policies? Then, ironically, the success of emerging markets to date may enable these countries to forge a self-reliant path that grinds their future catch-up process to a halt.

THE STAKES AHEAD

Nationalist instincts—a kind of economic schadenfreude, if you will—may cause some residents of rich countries to wish for a less ascendant developing world. Ostensibly, slower economic growth in upstart emerging economies could mean a more secure place for the developed world atop the economic food chain and perhaps lead to the return of manufacturing jobs that migrated overseas and better standards of living. Nothing, however, could be further from the truth. The future prosperity of countries like the United States, Germany, and Japan depends critically on the continued high performance of the BRICs and beyond. Cessation of catch-up by the emerging economies would make future economic conditions worse, not better, for the developed countries of the world.

In the aftermath of the Great Recession, unemployment in the developed world remains high—for example, roughly 8 percent in the United States as of June 2012 and 24 percent in Spain. For unemployment to fall from such high levels to historical norms, advanced economies will have to grow by 3 percent per year or more for a significant period of time. This will not be so easy to do. By definition, advanced countries are at the frontier of the world economy, with no scope for catch-up growth. In the absence of the potential for catch-up, they will need emerging economies to continue growing at a torrid clip. Although advanced economies have previously grown by 3 percent or more without the help of stellar performance by emerging markets, the two domestic channels through which higher growth might occur in the developed world—private-sector innovation and public-sector spending—face serious challenges this time around.

On the private side, a fragile banking system still recovering from the most severe financial crisis in almost a century remains reluctant to lend. Most immediately, banks and regulators in the United States must contend with the complex and unenviable task of implementing the Dodd-Frank Act, the landmark financial regulatory reform legislation signed into law by President Obama in May 2010. Financial reform will be a good thing for the US economy in the long run, but as the kinks get worked out in the short term, banks will remain cautious lenders at best. On the other side of the Atlantic, European banks remain highly exposed to the risky debts of Portugal, Ireland, Italy, Greece, and Spain. In short, it is hard to see a rapid return to profitable lending in the United States or Europe. Without such lending, private-sector innovation will suffer, acting as a drag on economic growth.

The public sectors of advanced economies are also not in a position to act as economic catalysts. With large national debts, record budget deficits, aging populations, rising health care costs, and looming entitlement obligations, such as Social Security, Medicare, and Medicaid in the United States, governments have little political latitude to generate growth through fiscal stimulus.

With private-sector innovation hampered by uncertainty and a lack of access to credit and the public sector limited in its ability to cut taxes or raise spending, exports must play a central role in helping advanced economies achieve and sustain the 3 percent growth they need to create jobs and reduce unemployment. As GDP expands in emerging economies, consumers in that part of the world will experience rising disposable incomes and increased purchasing power. Richer consumers in the developing world will demand more goods and services, some of which will take the form of imports from the advanced economies. In addition to helping create jobs, stronger export growth in advanced economies would help to alleviate the problem of global imbalances that contributed to the Great Recession of 2008–2009. "Global imbalances" is a fancy way of saying that rich countries are spending too much and saving too little, while developing countries are spending too little and saving too much. Greater exports by advanced countries will create jobs, raise the incomes of households in the developed world, and increase their capacity to save.

Although there is widespread agreement that the future economic prospects of the developed world depend heavily on the continuation of rapid growth in the BRICs and in other emerging markets as well, there could hardly be more disagreement about the role, if any, for the policy reform agenda in deepening and extending that growth. All informed observers recognize the centrality of capital, labor, and ideas.

The contentious point is whether the great catch-up of the last three decades—and the key to more in the future—occurred because of or in spite of the policy ideas of the IMF, the World Bank, and Western economic hegemony. For many citizens and policymakers in the developing world, nothing could be sweeter than the thought of telling the International Monetary Fund, the World Bank, and the World Trade Organization to "take this policy reform agenda and shove it," to paraphrase the 1977 hit song by Johnny Paycheck. The question is, what will happen if they do?

The best way to answer this question is to look at historical data. In Part II, we turn once more to the stock market to examine the effectiveness of each core policy. Taking into consideration country-specific circumstances, the analyses deliver a set of practical insights about where and when each individual reform promotes growth.

PART TWO

CHAPTER 5

AUSTERITY NOW?

FISCAL DISCIPLINE. THOSE TWO WORDS—THE FIRST ITEM on the original list of Washington Consensus policies and a major source of contention between the International Monetary Fund and those countries that seek its emergency financing—have caused more wailing and gnashing of teeth in the developing world than just about anything else. The standard arguments over what fiscal discipline means, to whom it should apply, and with what measure it should be meted out have moved from the Third World to the First World and taken center stage in the debate over the economic future of Europe.

On March 2, 2012, twenty-five states of the European Union signed the "Treaty on Stability, Coordination, and Governance in the Economic and Monetary Union" following months of negotiations driven by Germany and France. Better known as the "Fiscal Compact," the treaty takes effect on January 1, 2013, if the voters of at least twelve member countries have ratified it by that time. The main thrust of the agreement is that each party to the Compact will have to pass national legislation requiring that its central government's budget be balanced or in surplus. Failure to do so within a year of the Compact taking effect would trigger an automatic fine from the European Court of Justice.

To avoid falling afoul of the law, a country like Spain, whose deficit was 8.5 percent of GDP in 2011 and was expected to be 6.4 percent of GDP in 2012, would need to enact huge spending cuts and tax increases in the midst of 24 percent unemployment. Many countries besides Spain would require similarly drastic measures to comply. With joblessness in the Euro Area at an all-time high and cash-strapped families living hand to mouth, Germany's push for tighter fiscal policy across the continent is hardly welcome.

If the debate over the role of austerity in Europe was heated during the run-up to the signing of the Fiscal Compact, it rose to a veritable fever pitch with the election of François Hollande, France's new socialist president. Upon the announcement of his victory, President Hollande declared, "Austerity need not be Europe's fate." Since then, he has called for a European growth initiative and said that France would not ratify the Fiscal Compact without substantial changes.[1] German chancellor Angela Merkel has begged to differ, stating in no uncertain terms that "we in Germany are of the opinion, and so am I personally, that the fiscal pact is not negotiable."[2]

Irrespective of whether the Compact becomes law, there is no denying that there is a serious philosophical rift between the leaders of the two most important economies in Europe about the future of the Euro Area. Hollande wants stimulus in the form of government expenditure on infrastructure, industrial investment, and employment. Merkel insists on austerity now. Which approach would give European countries the best chance to stabilize their mounting debt, resolve the ongoing crisis, and start and sustain a robust economic recovery: stimulus, austerity—or neither?

Believe it or not, the historical struggle of developing countries to conquer high inflation has important parallels with the present-day travails of Europe (and the United States for that matter) and can help us understand how the definition of discipline we developed in Part One—sustained commitment to the future—can produce more sensible fiscal policy in a low-inflation environment.

Inflation and runaway debt are both consequences of governments' unwillingness to make disciplined choices with respect to spending and taxes. When deficits first enter the picture, they appear harmless enough and can, in fact, be quite useful. Temporary deficits tend to stimulate commercial activity and may provide a much-needed boost to the economy when times are hard. But temporary imbalances between spending and revenue tend to morph into a longer-lived phenomenon. Running large and persistent deficits is tantamount to playing with fire—eventually you get burned. How a country gets burned depends on how its government chooses to finance the revenue shortfall: through either debt—the accumulated bill of IOUs from past deficits—or monetization.

In the case of debt, for every nation there is a threshold of the ratio of debt to GDP at which the markets will simply say, "No more," and the government's ability to borrow from private sources will disappear. The critical threshold is typically lower for developing countries than for advanced nations, but the troubles of Greece, Italy, Portugal, and Spain make it abundantly clear that even developed countries face limits on the amount of debt they can accumulate before financial markets put an end to their ability to finance deficits.

Sovereign governments that choose to print money to pay their bills drive up inflation. In principle, this cannot happen in the Euro Area because individual countries do not have the authority to monetize their deficits. Nevertheless, many people, the Germans in particular, worry that the European Central Bank and the IMF will provide too much emergency money and allow the scourge of inflation to return to Europe. Since government expenditure in excess of revenues is the root cause of both debt and inflation crises, the two problems ultimately require the same solution—eradicating the fiscal deficit.

There are, however, many ways to proceed. The key question for any particular country is not whether to eliminate the deficit, but at what speed to do so, given its specific circumstances and the trade-offs involved. Under some scenarios, the benefits of austerity exceed the costs and make rapid, "cold-turkey" deficit reduction the optimal strategy for balancing the budget. But on other occasions, taking a gradual path toward eliminating the deficit actually constitutes the disciplined course of action.

How do we know which approach is the right one to take? Again, history is our best guide to the future. A relentless focus on deep and swift deficit reduction was the linchpin of the IMF stabilization programs that developing countries used to fight inflation in the 1970s, 1980s, and 1990s. Because fiscal austerity and IMF programs amount to largely the same approach, the collective response of developing-country economies to inflation stabilization efforts in the past provides a unique window onto the likely future impact of austerity in Europe today.

PAIN, THEN GAIN

Because inflation poses clear threats to a modern economy, it is tempting to conclude that a dogged commitment to reducing it—a process that economists refer to interchangeably as "stabilization" or "disinflation"—would be an easy win for policymakers who adopt the motto, to paraphrase Cato, "Inflation must fall!" If reducing inflation were costless, then this would be an obvious rallying cry indeed. The problem is that stabilization, like anything else worth achieving, involves trade-offs. The adjustments required to reduce inflation—in other words, tighter fiscal and monetary policy—can inflict painful short-run costs on the economy before delivering long-run benefits.

For instance, fiscal consolidation in the form of expenditure cuts and tax increases reduces the amount of overall spending in the economy because governments in all countries consume significant quantities of goods and services. As public spending falls, inventories rise and firms cut back on production, investment, and hiring. As hiring falls, unemployment rises and households have less income, causing private spending to fall as well. Tighter monetary policy has a similar impact. When the central bank slows the flow of money into the economy, interest rates rise and the cost of borrowing increases for businesses and households, further reducing investment and consumption.

Policymakers believe that the slowdown of economic activity and the rise in unemployment are necessary to reduce inflation.[3] It is this painful reality of stabilization programs that leads economists to talk about the "sacrifice ratio" associated with disinflation. The sacrifice ratio is the percentage-point increase in the unemployment rate caused by a stabilization program divided by the percentage-point decline in inflation. In plain English, the sacrifice ratio measures the number of short-run units of pain the economy must endure per unit of long-run gain.

The sacrifice ratio is a poignant reminder that stabilization involves trade-offs. As damaging as inflation may be to an economy, it is only worth reducing if the benefits from doing so outweigh the costs. How can we tell if this is the case? The answer to this question follows directly from the concept of present value discussed in Chapter 1.

The stock market internalizes both the short- and long-run effects of disinflation on the economy—that is, the expectation of slower growth and higher interest rates in the short run depresses present values, but the prospect of the long-run rewards exerts a countervailing force. Once the difficult times pass and a lower inflation rate takes hold, the economy grows faster and produces a larger stream of earnings. Reduced inflation also delivers lower interest rates and less volatile earnings. If the expected long-run benefits of reducing inflation outweigh the short-run costs, then the aggregate stock market index will rise when a country's government announces a stabilization program. If the expected costs outweigh the benefits, the market will fall. If the net anticipated effect is a wash, there will be little to no market reaction. The story of Brazil in 1994 provides a useful first example of this kind of cost-benefit analysis.

Keeping It Real in Rio

Following the onset of the Third World Debt Crisis in 1982, more than a decade's worth of Brazilian presidents failed to bring about economic stability. Unwilling or unable to close serial fiscal deficits and cut off from external financing as a result of the crisis, administration after administration monetized the financing gap until inflation became a permanent resident of the four-digit stratosphere. Figure 5.1 demonstrates the role of the deficit in Brazil's epic struggle with inflation. The solid line, plotted on the left-hand scale, is the fiscal deficit as a fraction of GDP.[4] The dashed line, plotted on the right-hand scale, is the rate of consumer-price inflation.

While the monetization of deficits triggered high inflation in Brazil during the 1980s and early 1990s, another less obvious culprit helped ensure its longevity. Brazil, like many other Latin American countries in that era, set future wages and prices on the basis of the inflation rate in previous years—a practice known as "backward-looking indexation." Backward-looking indexation embedded past inflation into future wage and price increases, creating both persistence in inflation and harmful movements in relative prices like the real wage. So, even though deficits were a central reason why Brazil failed to stabilize inflation on seven consecutive tries between 1983 and 1992, backward-looking indexation prolonged high inflation and exacerbated the problems it caused.

In July 1993, Finance Minister Fernando Henrique Cardoso unveiled "Plano Real," a stabilization program designed to close the deficit and break the link with past inflation. The first phase of the program entailed budget cuts, stricter tax collection, and the end of monetization.

The second phase occurred in March 1994, when Cardoso's economic team announced that it was phasing out the old, inflation-debased currency (the *cruzeiro*). Introducing a new currency was old hat—at that point Brazil had undergone three previous changes in the

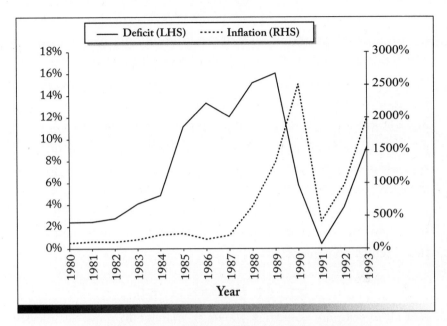

**FIGURE 5.I: BUDGET DEFICITS IN BRAZIL
DROVE INFLATION**

currency since 1986. The radical new step of the Plano Real was the
way in which it introduced the *unidade real de valor* (URV) (real value
unit) as the economy's new principal unit of account. The government
required the posting of all prices and wages in URVs and made it clear
that on the first of July it would convert all URV-based prices into
real, the new currency whose official trading value would be at par
with the US dollar.

Because the *real* effectively operated alongside the old currency for
four months, workers, employers, and firms had an opportunity to adjust prices and wages in line with their expectations about the future
rather than the past. This made a large difference. The Plano Real
triggered a series of wage and price adjustments predicated on the expectation of lower future inflation that set in motion a self-reinforcing
process of declining inflation.

By eliminating backward indexation, Brazil managed to substantially reduce the short-run costs of stabilization, and the stock market responded accordingly. In the year leading up to the introduction of the new currency, the Bovespa Index experienced cumulative abnormal returns of 75 percent in real dollar terms. And inflation dropped like a stone—from 3000 percent in 1994 to 66 percent in 1995 to 16 percent in 1996 and 7 percent in 1997. In a short period of time, Brazil moved from high inflation to single digits, and it has remained there ever since, with an average inflation rate of about 6 percent per year. As a result of the fall in inflation, the increase in growth that ensued, and the implementation of antipoverty measures, poverty in Brazil fell by 20 percent.[5]

STUCK IN SANTIAGO

Not all developing countries, however, manage to move seamlessly from high to low inflation. When Augusto Pinochet violently seized power in 1973, Chile's inflation rate was well into the triple digits. The junta's rise stemmed in no small part from the disastrous economic management of the Allende government it overthrew. During Salvador Allende's brief stint in office (1970 to 1973), the fiscal deficit averaged 16.1 percent of GDP, inflation was 150 percent, and the country grew by a paltry 0.5 percent per year. (It is also worth noting that Allende's decision to nationalize much of industry and seize the commanding heights of the economy bore a similarity to the policies of Michael Manley, Jamaica's prime minister in the early 1970s.)

Almost immediately after taking power, the Pinochet regime enacted an orthodox stabilization program, slashing the fiscal deficit to 5.1 percent of GDP from 1974 to 1976 and actually running small fiscal surpluses between 1977 and 1981. Unlike Brazil's Plano Real in 1994, the Chilean program did not eliminate the backward-looking indexation of wages that had informally been in place since 1974 and that became official with the passage of the "Plan Laboral" (the "Labor Plan") in 1979. The failure to rid the economy of backward indexation was a major reason why, although the Pinochet government managed to bring down high inflation, Chile got stuck with moderate inflation on the order of 20 percent per year.

MODERATE INFLATION
IS NO PICNIC EITHER

Indexation and the attendant persistence of moderate inflation had serious ramifications for the international sector of Chile's economy. As part of their stabilization strategy, the Chilean authorities limited the speed of depreciation of the exchange rate through a program of publicized exchange-rate targets called the *tablita*. Doing so dampened the rise in the prices of imported goods, limited their impact on the consumer price index, and helped bring the inflation rate down from high to moderate. Inflation persisted at moderate levels instead of dropping to single digits, however, and the depreciation of the exchange rate under the *tablita* did not keep pace with the rate of domestic price increases, making Chilean goods more expensive to foreigners. Exports fell, imports grew, and the trade deficit expanded from 1.8 percent of GDP in 1977 to 10.3 percent in 1981.

The large and growing trade deficits increased Chile's foreign borrowing requirements at precisely the same time that banks around the world were pulling in their loans to developing countries. To obtain the money it needed to continue servicing its external debt, Chile turned to the IMF and implemented austerity measures under the auspices of three official agreements from 1983 to 1989.

The Chilean stock market took a rather dim view of the government's decision to enact austerity measures in the midst of moderate inflation and a highly indexed economy. Cumulative abnormal returns were negative in the twelve-month period preceding each of Chile's three IMF agreements in the 1980s, and the average cumulative abnormal return across all three episodes was negative 87 percent. Although the agreements helped to stabilize Chile's external debt, real GDP fell sharply in 1982 and did not return to its pre-recession level until 1986. The agreements also failed to reduce inflation. Inflation was 27 percent per year when Chile signed its first IMF agreement in 1983 and 26 percent in 1990, a year after its last agreement.

From Latin America
to the World

The market's starkly different response to the stabilization of high versus moderate inflation is not unique to Brazil and Chile. Figure 5.2 illustrates the collective stabilization experiences of twenty-one emerging nations with the two varieties of inflation between 1973 and 1994: twenty-five episodes of high inflation with a median inflation rate of 118 percent per year, and fifty-six episodes of moderate inflation with a median inflation rate of 15 percent.[6] The solid line indicates that in anticipation of stabilization programs directed at high inflation, the average national stock market experienced cumulative abnormal returns of 44 percent. In contrast, the dashed line indicates that in anticipation of stabilization programs directed at moderate inflation, the stock market experienced cumulative abnormal returns of negative 24 percent.

To give the data a little more texture, it's worth noting just how often stabilizations fail. Let's define a successful stabilization program in the case of high inflation as one that causes inflation to fall below 40 percent and stay there for two or more years. Similarly, we can define a successful stabilization program in the case of moderate inflation as one that causes inflation to fall below 10 percent and stay there for two or more years. Using these criteria, Argentina failed to stabilize high inflation eight times in fifteen years before finally succeeding on the ninth try. Brazil tried and failed seven times before slaying high inflation with the Plano Real. Overall, the average country attempted four stabilizations—one roughly every five years—and only twelve of the eighty-one attempts succeeded. Interestingly, the rate of success in high-inflation episodes is greater than in the moderate-inflation cases.

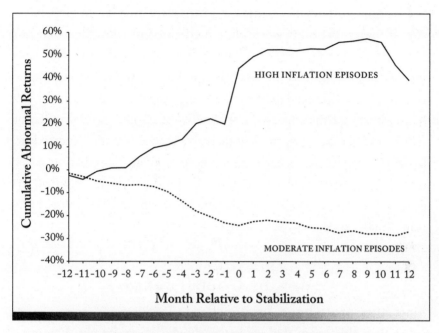

FIGURE 5.2: THE STOCK MARKET RESPONDS POSITIVELY TO STABILIZATION PROGRAMS DIRECTED AT HIGH INFLATION

Seven of twenty-five attempts at stabilizing high inflation (28 percent) succeed, whereas the number is less than 10 percent (five of fifty-six) in the moderate-inflation cases. Because stabilization attempts fail with great frequency, one can think of the stock market responses depicted in Figure 5.2 roughly as the true net present value of a successful stabilization program multiplied by the probability of the program being followed through to completion. With a 28 percent chance of success, the fact that the market soars by 44 percent in anticipation of stabilization programs directed at high inflation suggests that people expect really good things to happen if the program succeeds. Analogous logic suggests that the 24 percent fall in the stock market may understate how much value people anticipate being destroyed by programs directed at reducing moderate inflation.

Looking at Figure 5.2 tempts us to conclude that it's an obvious result. If high inflation is worse than moderate inflation, then reducing it surely must bring larger benefits. But remember the sacrifice ratio. Because stabilization is not free, the total cost of reducing high inflation might well exceed that of reducing moderate inflation. So it is not a given that the expected net benefits of stabilizing high inflation will be greater. Second, the key question is whether the expected net benefits are positive in each case. The interesting observation is not just that the expected net benefits of reducing high inflation are greater, but that the expected net benefit of reducing moderate inflation actually appears to be negative.

GRADUALISM
VERSUS COLD TURKEY

Since attempts to bring down moderate inflation appear to destroy value, does this mean that countries should ignore it? No. The question is not whether to reduce moderate inflation, but how. All fifty-six attempts to reduce moderate inflation depicted in Figure 5.2 took place under the auspices of IMF programs that relied on traditional methods of stabilization under which countries typically devalue the currency, cut the deficit, and curtail the growth rate of the money supply in one fell swoop. What Figure 5.2 tells us, therefore, is that the market thinks that "cold-turkey" methods of stabilization destroy value when implemented in the midst of moderate inflation.

Looking at the impact of Chile's homegrown stabilization in the early 1990s, on the other hand, illustrates the value of a gradual approach. Following three IMF programs and a decade of little progress in reducing inflation to single digits, in 1990 the Central Bank of Chile (CBC) embarked on a gradual course to rid the country of moderate inflation.[7] Chile could have tried another, perhaps more extreme stabilization program in an attempt to quickly wring moderate inflation out of the economy once and for all, but in the words of

Vittorio Corbo, former governor of the CBC, "Considering Chile's widespread backward indexation practice, it was understood that rapid disinflation could entail high output costs. . . . In order to minimize this risk, the Central Bank of Chile opted for a very gradual approach to stabilization."[8]

Specifically, in September 1990, the CBC publicly announced its intention that as of the coming December it would adopt an official inflation target and would tighten monetary policy as necessary to achieve it. The first target in a series, set for the period of December 1990 to December 1991, was an annual inflation rate of 15 to 20 percent. Over the decade from 1991 to 2001, the CBC reduced the target by an average of 1.5 percentage points per year. By publicly articulating an explicit goal and putting its credibility at stake through an equally public commitment to use monetary policy to achieve it, the CBC managed to mitigate the impact of past inflation on future wage and price increases, breaking the hold of backward-looking indexation, de facto if not de jure.

The stock market looked favorably upon the CBC's gradualist approach to reducing moderate inflation. In anticipation of the program's future impact, the stock market experienced cumulative abnormal returns of more than 100 percent over the twelve-month period preceding implementation—a markedly different forecast than in the case of the three cold-turkey austerity programs implemented under the auspices of IMF agreements in the 1980s (see Figure 5.3). The sanguine stock market forecast proved to be accurate. By 1995, inflation had declined from moderate to low (where it has remained ever since) and Chile's average GDP growth rate between 1990 and 1998 was more than twice that of the previous decade.[9]

FOCUS AND FLEXIBILITY

As policymakers seek to influence the future course of their country's economy, they need to weigh the costs and benefits of stabilization.

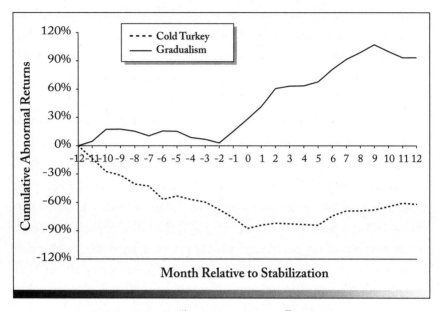

FIGURE 5.3: "COLD-TURKEY" VERSUS GRADUALIST APPROACHES TO MODERATE INFLATION IN CHILE

Austerity measures initiated in the midst of high inflation are likely to create value. In a moderate-inflation context, they appear to do just the opposite. Moderate inflation calls for a vigilant but more gradual approach that is grounded in the right mix of homegrown stabilization policies and tailored to a country-specific understanding of the root causes of inflation. Given that the inflation rate for the Euro Area in 2012 was less than 3 percent, the implications seem relatively straightforward: instead of attempting to balance budgets immediately, which would require a drastic swing in investment and consumption and exacerbate the region's economic woes, the Euro Area countries could take a page out of the Chilean playbook and adopt a long-term target for fiscal deficits along with clear and credible measures to help deliver on those goals.

To its credit, the IMF took steps in the direction of endorsing a more gradual approach to fiscal adjustment as early as 2010. In June of that year, two IMF officials, Olivier Blanchard, chief economist, and Carlo Cotarelli, the director of fiscal affairs, wrote a blog post, "Ten Commandments for Fiscal Adjustment in Advanced Economies," that urged policymakers to lean in the direction of gradualist versus cold-turkey adjustments.[10] The influence of their work is readily apparent in a May 2012 speech given by IMF managing director Christine Lagarde. Speaking in Zurich, she praised countries for reducing their deficits by about one percentage point of GDP per year—a far cry from the reductions of up to five percentage points that would be required under the Fiscal Compact—and urged countries to stick to fiscal measures instead of fiscal targets if growth should turn out to be weaker than expected.[11] In other words, she urged them to be flexible.

Although the IMF's position on gradual deficit reduction in Europe is eminently sensible, the organization must communicate clearly to its non-Western stakeholders that its newfound flexibility is not an ad hoc exception for European countries that wield outsized influence but rather a fundamental change in its thinking toward fiscal adjustment in advanced *and* developing countries. When financial markets lose confidence in the policies of a nation, it may have no choice but to embrace tough measures to regain access to international capital markets, but the IMF should take seriously the evidence—from the stock market and elsewhere—that a gradual path of deficit reduction is also appropriate beyond Europe and do what it can to help facilitate disciplined policies and smooth adjustments.

A gradualist approach does not signal a lack of commitment—it is about altering the speed of progress toward a specified fiscal target, not about changing the desired destination or sense of purpose. Moving more slowly toward the target can be a valuable tactic as part of a larger growth strategy. The key point is not to balance the budget as quickly as possible but to adopt measures that credibly place public finances on a sustainable path that keeps the specter of inflation and debt crises at bay. The resulting stability enables governments to focus their time and energy on policies to increase productivity.

The lessons of stabilization extend beyond specific questions about how quickly to reduce the deficit. Successful economic reforms often require short-run pain to deliver long-run gains. Creative and clever approaches may improve the cost-benefit trade-offs, but in the end leaders must be willing to make—and stick with—hard decisions that can take many years to reach fruition. In an age when electronic communication has encouraged people to expect "real-time" results, it bears emphasizing that Brazil's robust economy and attendant rise on the world stage would not have been possible without the courageous decisions made by Cardoso—first as finance minister and then as president—almost two decades ago, nor without sustained commitment to those decisions by the successive administrations of President Lula da Silva.

Brazil's rise to international prominence reminds us that stabilization also has an impact on the international components of a country's economy, such as the trade balance, the current account, and foreign debt. Given the increasingly integrated nature of the world economy, once governments achieve a measure of macroeconomic stability, their attention naturally turns to policies directed at the cross-border exchange of goods and services.

CHAPTER 6

THE TERMS OF TRADE

WHEN I WAS A THIRD-GRADER AT THE GLENLEIGH SCHOOL in Jamaica, I sat next to Gary McKenzie every day at lunch. Gary and I got along fine, but the true source of our affinity lay as much in food as it did in friendship. Gary's family owned a restaurant, so he always had cooked leftovers for lunch: jerk chicken, rice and peas, and steamed vegetables. My dad worked for Cadbury's, so I always had chocolate (to go along with my pedestrian peanut butter sandwiches). I loved jerk chicken and had more chocolate than I could handle. Gary craved chocolate and had a surfeit of chicken. It didn't take long for us to work out the price of chicken in terms of chocolate.

As it is with elementary school lunches, so it goes with international economics. Countries trade with each other—albeit usually for money instead of in kind—for the same reasons kids do. People of all nations want to consume a broad range of products. Variety is the spice of life, and differences create opportunities for mutually beneficial exchange.

There are many kinds of differences across countries that make international trade advantageous to all parties involved. Consider natural resources. Tropical countries that receive large amounts of rain grow bananas and send them to countries that have more temperate climates and produce lots of wheat. A country like Russia could spend billions of rubles building heated greenhouses to replicate tropical conditions and try to grow enough bananas to feed its population. But trade creates an opportunity to do more with the same amount of resources. It is more efficient for Russia to sell wheat abroad and use the proceeds from those exports to buy bananas from Ecuador. The average number of rubles Russia spends for each banana it imports is far less than the average cost it would bear for each banana grown in a Russian greenhouse.

Ecuador has what economists call a "comparative advantage" in bananas because it produces them at a lower opportunity cost than Russia. Russia has a comparative advantage in wheat. By definition, everybody has comparative advantage in something.

The concept of comparative advantage easily extends from the description of any two goods to entire economies. As discussed in Chapter 4, a country uses capital, labor, and ideas to produce the goods and services that constitute its gross domestic product. Because wages are low in labor-abundant countries, they have a comparative advantage in the production of labor-intensive goods. Capital-abundant countries have a low cost of capital and thus a comparative advantage in the production of capital-intensive goods.

The total amount of goods and services that a country can produce in a sustainable fashion given its pool of capital, labor, and ideas is called "potential output." A country can expand its potential output by building up its capital stock and labor force and by adopting policies that encourage more efficient deployment of capital and labor. One such policy is free trade, which enables countries to specialize in producing those things in which they have comparative advantage and to trade for things they make less efficiently. Free trade allows labor-abundant countries like Vietnam to focus on producing labor-intensive goods (like garments) that it can make at low cost and export to the rest of the world to earn the foreign exchange it needs to import capital-intensive goods (like tractors) that countries such as Germany make at lower cost. Put another way, free trade allows countries to make the most of what they have.

Besides providing access to cheaper goods and raising productivity, free trade also brings other benefits. Many products, such as the electronic microcircuits that are used in everything from computers to security surveillance equipment, are subject to "economies of scale," meaning that the cost of making each additional unit of the product declines as the total number of units made increases. Trade with the rest of the world allows countries to exploit economies of scale and expands the potential size of the market for which they produce.[1]

Similarly, the range of products that lie within the ambit of a country's comparative advantage is typically wider than the domestic market can support. South Korea, for example, did not have color broadcasting until 1980, but began producing and exporting color television sets in 1974.[2] Because world demand for goods exceeds and at times is more advanced than domestic demand, free trade allows countries to produce profitably a wider range of goods than would be possible in the absence of exchange with the rest of the world. The smaller the country, the more important the potential benefits of economies of scale and scope that come from free trade, more efficient resource allocation, and access to the global marketplace. Moreover, productive workers need jobs that demand their skills, and the world market is an important potential outlet for the goods produced by a country's labor force.

But in making the most of the world market, countries need to avoid falling into the trade trap—the intellectual pitfall of believing that exports are good, imports are bad, and running a large trade surplus is the key to prosperity. From 1995 to 2007, the world economy experienced one of the most rapid periods of growth in human history, and yet the global trade balance was exactly the same as it has always been—zero. Unless we start trading with Mars, the world will never run a trade surplus.

The key to prosperity lies not in the balance of trade but in the power of productivity. Free trade is good for the world because it unleashes the power of comparative advantage writ large. Imports allow countries to consume the things that it is not in their interest to make. Exports enable them to earn the income they need to pay for the imports. As comparative advantage kicks in and workers move into sectors of the economy where they are more productive, their incomes rise and they demand more and different kinds of imports; that demand, in turn, drives up the incomes of workers in countries that sell those goods.

This virtuous cycle of mutually beneficial exchange and rising national incomes currently stands in jeopardy. Opposition to free trade, and to imports in particular, was once the province of developing nations. Now it is largely the rich countries that balk at further dismantling of the barriers to trade. Because trade liberalization creates winners and losers, the prospect of opening up generates opposition. Calls for protectionism, in both the developed and developing worlds, are a natural response. But the developing world's experience with easing trade restrictions reveals that living standards increase in countries whose leaders resist protectionism and make a lasting commitment to policies that harness the power of both exports *and* imports.

IT TAKES TWO
TO TANGO

In much of Africa, Latin America, and parts of Asia during the 1950s, 1960s, and 1970s, the trade trap took the form of an import substitution strategy based on the premise that keeping foreign goods out of their local markets would enable developing countries to nurture infant industries, become self-sufficient, and prosper. But the strategy neither led to self-reliance nor helped raise living standards. As many adherents of import substitution would learn in the coming decades, there are a variety of ways in which restricting the flow of imports into a developing country actually undermines its productivity and ability to export. They would learn, in other words, that it takes two to tango.

High tariffs raised the local price of imported goods, encouraging local businesses to shift scarce resources toward the production of importable goods such as cars and washing machines and away from more efficient, lower-cost industries. Because many of these lower-cost industries tended to be in the exportable goods sector (think beef in Argentina), tariffs unintentionally biased production toward a small domestic customer base and prevented countries from exploiting the economies of scale and scope inherent in producing for a large global market.

Higher tariffs also reduced the demand for imports and the foreign exchange needed to pay for them. The fall in demand for foreign exchange increased the value of the local currency vis-à-vis other currencies like the US dollar, a process called "appreciation of the exchange rate." As the exchange rate appreciated, these countries' goods became increasingly expensive and less attractive on international markets, thus undermining prospects for new exports, weakening the performance of traditional exports, and making infant industries even less competitive. Furthermore, tariffs on important inputs into the production process, such as agricultural and industrial machinery, made it more expensive to produce manufactured goods, exacerbating the competitiveness problem caused by an appreciating currency. When certain kinds of inputs, such as chemical catalysts in Indian fertilizers, were made subject to strict quotas or simply banned outright, industry productivity and quality suffered.[3]

Import bans on production inputs like machines and the equipment needed to service them hindered developing economies in important, unintended ways. Because 70 percent of the world's machine imports come from the handful of industrial countries that account for virtually all of the world's research and development (R&D),

prohibiting the import of capital goods also curtailed the flow of new ideas into countries that desperately needed them in order to grow. By restricting imports, countries lost out on new and existing export opportunities and inhibited investment that could have increased the productivity of their workers.

Thirty years of import substitution brought little progress to the developing world. Tariffs distorted production, and the byzantine web of quotas and licenses—famously, the "license Raj" in India, which required firms to obtain official permission to expand into new product lines or upgrade capacity—created systems that encouraged people to make money through corruption rather than creativity. Instead of engaging in productive entrepreneurial activity, people spent their time trying to circumvent barriers and concoct schemes to gain control of the sale of state-sanctioned import licenses, and the artificial scarcity of goods led to the creation of black markets.

In the absence of foreign competition, local businesses across the developing world had no incentive to innovate, cut costs, or produce better products. Consequently, "creative destruction"—the process that drives knowledge creation by encouraging the entry of efficient firms and the exit of inefficient ones—all but disappeared. Consumers were stuck with inferior goods at high prices, companies suffered with old equipment and outdated technology, and governments had to confront the reality of an experiment gone badly wrong.

A Rising Tide (Eventually) Lifts All Boats

The failure of import substitution was disappointing—and expensive. In the aftermath of the failed experiment, countries came to the World Bank in the 1980s asking for money to help rebuild their economies. The Bank seized the opportunity to push an aggressive trade liberalization agenda, extending structural adjustment loans to countries if and only if they agreed to reduce barriers to trade. As a result, developing countries are now substantially more open than ever before. In 1980, 25 percent of the world's countries had open trade policies; by the year 2000, that number stood at 73 percent.[4] Today, by a number of measures, developing countries actually trade more with the rest of the world than do their rich-country counterparts.[5]

In theory, opening a closed country to trade allows capital and labor to move from sectors where they were used inefficiently to sectors where the formerly closed country has comparative advantage. Figure 6.1 provides a simplified visual illustration of the point by tracing out the expected evolution of GDP per capita over time in two imaginary economies that are identical in every respect except that one is open to free trade (Country O) and the other is closed (Country C). Because Country O makes more efficient use of its resources, it has a higher initial level of GDP per capita than Country C. For simplicity's sake, we assume that the initial growth rate in both countries is the same so that the income gap between the two countries remains constant.

At time 0, the government of Country C liberalizes trade. As resource allocation improves, a period of catch-up growth ensues—C expands more rapidly, narrowing the income gap with O. As the gap shrinks, growth in C eventually returns to its preliberalization rate. Although the catch-up rates of growth experienced by C during its transition to an open economy do not last forever, as a result of trade liberalization Country C now has a permanently higher level of GDP per capita than it would have had if it remained closed.

Pictures are nice, but facts trump theory in the world of politics. If the real-world impact of opening a country to free trade bears any resemblance to the illustration in Figure 6.1, then theoretically the long-run benefits of trade liberalization will outweigh any temporary costs: new jobs will be created for workers displaced by liberalization, and profit opportunities will arise for owners who had to close their

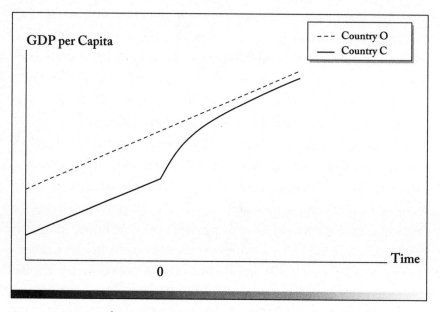

**FIGURE 6.1: TRADE LIBERALIZATION INCREASES
GDP PER CAPITA**

factories in the face of foreign imports. Does the theory hold up to
scrutiny? Leaders will not expend political capital for freer trade without convincing evidence that trade liberalization actually produces
these results. Unfortunately, much of the evidence available to date is
misleading.

OPENNESS VERSUS OPENING

In the year 2000, economists Francisco Rodríguez and Dani Rodrik
looked carefully at the major studies of trade liberalization and concluded that its record is not so good.[6] Identifying deficient empirical
methodologies and errors related to measuring trade openness
throughout a number of seminal papers, the authors offered careful
rebuttals and alternative explanations for the key findings that supported a link between fewer barriers and growth. They found no reli-

able evidence that lowering trade barriers improves economic performance in any significant way.

In fact, virtually all of the studies that Rodríguez and Rodrik
looked at focused on the question of whether countries that are open
to trade grow faster than countries that are closed. This is the wrong
question. Comparative advantage does not predict that open countries
will grow faster than closed countries. It predicts that a closed country
will grow faster for a significant period of time as a result of opening
up. In terms of Figure 6.1, the relevant comparison is not between the
growth rates of Country O and Country C, but between the growth
rates of C before and after trade liberalization.[7] In short, the studies
examined by Rodríguez and Rodrik did not test for the transitional
effect of catch-up growth predicted by comparative advantage, so
there is little surprise that they did not find one.

Eight years after the Rodríguez and Rodrik survey, economists Romain Wacziarg and Karen Welch did ask the right question and
reached very different conclusions about the impact of trade liberalization.[8] Wacziarg and Welch found that in the twenty-year period
following trade liberalizations, countries grew about 1.5 percentage
points faster than in the previous twenty years, with the largest increase in growth rates coming in the first five years after liberalization.
This is no small effect. The average citizen of a country that started
with a GDP per capita of $10,000 and experienced an extra 1.5 percentage points of growth per year for twenty years as a result of trade
liberalization would be about $3,500 richer than they would have
been in the absence of the change.

STOCKS AND TRADE

Making a distinction between a country's openness to trade and the
process of its opening up to trade moves us closer to understanding
the impact of trade on growth—yet obstacles remain. The bump in
growth rates that some developing countries experience after opening

up may inspire confidence in other nations considering the same course of action. But they should bear in mind the possibility that the increase in growth rates over a five- to twenty-year horizon is the result of events not directly related to trade liberalization. Governments undergoing trade liberalization are likely to have implemented other policy changes as well or to have experienced events beyond their control. When looking at an economy over a period as long as twenty years, how much confidence can policymakers really have that trade liberalization and not some other factor is responsible for faster growth?

Again, the stock market can help. When a government announces its intent to liberalize trade, the aggregate stock price response in the months between the announcement and the implementation provides a forecast that circumvents some of the problems associated with using data on GDP growth to evaluate the policy change twenty years after the fact. The approach is far from perfect, but extracting a long-run forecast from the market's more immediate response provides a cleaner measure of the expected impact of trade policy.

Pinning down the timing of the change in trade policy, however, is a challenge. The studies reviewed by Rodríguez and Rodrik and by Wacziarg and Welch provided the year that trade liberalizations took place. This is sufficient information when working with annual data like GDP. However, because stock prices respond rapidly to news, it is critical to have a sense of the month in which the change occurred. If a country liberalized trade in January 1987, the market might have learned of the impending policy change as early as the middle of the previous year and reacted to it right away. If we look only at stock returns in 1987, they are likely to miss the very market reaction they seek to capture. Using a twelve-month window before the implementation date addresses this concern.

Of all the developing countries one might consider, a total of just fourteen have both verifiable trade liberalization dates and reliable stock market data: Argentina, Brazil, Chile, Colombia, India, Indonesia, Jordan, Mexico, Pakistan, the Philippines, South Korea, Thailand, Turkey, and Venezuela. The small sample size is a trade-off associated with the stock market approach: one gets a clearer lens through which to view events of interest, but fewer events to observe.

The liberalization dates for the fourteen countries run from as early as January 1968 in the case of South Korea to September 1989 for Turkey.[9] The average country in the sample experienced cumulative abnormal returns of 60 percent in real dollar terms within twelve months of the government's decision to liberalize trade. Thirteen of the fourteen countries experienced positive stock market reactions, and Argentina, Indonesia, and Turkey amassed cumulative abnormal returns in excess of 100 percent.[10]

As noted earlier, when countries introduce trade reforms many other changes to the economy are usually taking place or being discussed at the same time. How do we know if the change in trade policy is responsible for the revaluation of stocks? In the case of stabilization programs, this is less of a worry: as we saw in the previous chapter, high inflation is so disruptive to the economy that one of the reasons for stabilizing it is to create the conditions required for other reforms such as trade liberalization to succeed. Since trade liberalizations typically take place after the stabilization process is already under way, there is a distinct possibility that stocks are revalued because of concurrent reforms. Econometric work finds a positive market reaction to trade liberalization even after controlling for this concern.[11]

SWITCHING IN SEOUL

If you ask most people why trade liberalization helps countries grow faster, they will probably give you an answer straight from the trade trap: opening up to imports makes other countries more willing to buy your exports. There is some truth to this view, but it is a half-truth at best. South Korea, one of the most remarkable turnaround stories in modern economic history, provides a case in point.

Depending on how you count, there are roughly 180 countries in the world, and as Nobel Laureate economist Michael Spence points out in his book *The Next Convergence,* only thirteen of them have ever managed to grow by an average of 7 percent or more over a period of twenty-five years. Korea is one of those thirteen. It is no secret that an export-led strategy contributed greatly to Korea's growth. What people fail to appreciate, however, is the critical role that the lifting of import restrictions—plus a dash of stabilization—played in the strategy that transformed Korea from a stagnant economy into a soaring success.

During the 1950s, close to 90 percent of Korea's exports were primary products like copper, graphite, tungsten, and talc. Eager to change the country's pattern of trade, the government introduced a dizzying array of import restrictions, quotas, tariffs, licenses, and other protectionist measures designed to spur a manufacturing sector that could compete with and supplant foreign imports.[12] For reasons outlined earlier in this chapter, the strategy did not work. The country grew slowly, inflation soared, and as the exchange rate was held fixed for long periods of time, the increasing overvaluation of what is known as the "real exchange rate" damaged exports and undermined growth.

The real exchange rate is another type of relative price (recall the real wage from Chapter 3). It is the price of goods produced abroad, measured in local currency, relative to the price of goods produced at home. Korea's real exchange rate vis-à-vis the United States is the number of baskets of Korean goods it takes to buy a single basket of US goods. Americans and Koreans do not consume identical items, but as long as the composition of their baskets is comparable—food, clothing, shelter, and energy—the real exchange rate provides a useful cross-country comparison of costs. Just as a decrease in the Korean exchange rate increases the value of the *won* in terms of dollars, a decrease in Korea's real exchange rate means that its goods have become more expensive in relation to US goods.

In an efficient economy, the real exchange rate stays roughly constant so that a country's goods do not become overly cheap or expensive and its trade balance is sustainable. During rapid inflation, however, the consumer price index usually rises faster than the exchange rate, causing a harmful downward trend in the real exchange rate. The decline in the real exchange rate reduces the number of local baskets required to buy a foreign basket, a phenomenon known as an "appreciation" of the real exchange rate, or a "real appreciation."

Extended periods of real appreciation make a country's goods increasingly expensive and uncompetitive with foreign goods—exports fall. On the flip side, foreign goods become increasingly cheap in comparison to domestic goods—imports rise. The combination of falling exports and increasing imports typically leads to slow growth plus an unsustainable trade deficit.

This was Korea's situation in the mid-1950s, when the US Congress concluded that "there was little or no hope for sustained growth in South Korea," and World Bank studies stated that "industrial growth in Korea was not feasible."[13] Prospects looked grim. Faced with slow growth, rapid inflation, and low expectations from the international community, the Korean government confronted the shortcomings of import substitution in 1964 and changed course.

Under the leadership of President Park Chung-hee, Korea began liberalizing trade. Korea did not simply fling its economy wide open—the country retained high import tariffs on a wide range of items from agricultural products to computer equipment—but the authorities were wise enough to recognize the necessity of imports for Korea's economic development. They also paid close attention to the composition of goods coming into the country.

Initially, Korean officials kept a short but growing "positive" list of permissible capital items. In 1967 they replaced it with a "negative" list system in which all items not on the list were automatically allowed. This selective approach to trade liberalization made it easier to import goods that embodied foreign technology—both intermediate inputs used in production, like ball bearings, and capital goods such as transport equipment and machinery. Furthermore, local firms began to reverse-engineer the imported products; Korea's auto industry is a good example of the result.[14] Korea first imported car engines, then moved to producing them under license; now the country boasts its own automobile designs.[15] Beyond motor vehicles, Korean companies jump-started the cement, paper, and steel industries by importing turnkey plants and assimilating the technologies embodied in the ready-made facilities.

As an important complement to its import liberalization agenda, in 1964 the Korean government also decided to reduce the fiscal deficit and devalue the *won*. A country cannot have a successful export-led growth strategy with an overvalued currency that makes its goods so expensive that foreigners don't want to buy them. By counteracting the tendency of Korea's remaining trade barriers to cause real exchange rate appreciation, the devaluation of the currency restored the competitiveness of Korean goods on the world market and enabled Korea to develop a world-class manufacturing sector that now makes products ranging from semiconductors to prefabricated desalinization plants.

Korea's policies also demonstrate that imports and exports work together in a rapidly growing economy. The country's exports increased from 4.8 percent of GDP in 1963 to 34 percent in 1980. Imports as a fraction of GDP rose from 15.9 percent in 1963 to 41.4 percent in 1980.[16] Note that Korea's trade balance was negative in both 1963 and in 1980. In fact, from 1965 to 1990, Korea's GDP grew by 7.1 percent per year, with the country running trade deficits for almost that entire period. The Korean government's willingness to admit the shortcomings of its import substitution policies and change tack radically altered the country's economic trajectory. In 1960 Korea was poorer than Jamaica, with a GDP per capita of US$1,100 and going nowhere fast. By 2005 Korea's average standard of living had increased twelvefold.

Critics of economic reform often cite Korea's success as evidence that free-market policy changes are not necessary for growth. The Korean government unquestionably played a significant role in the country's rise to economic prominence. In the words of the late economist Alice Amsden, "Every major shift in industrial diversification in the 1960s and 1970s was instigated by the state."[17] Be that as it may, the key element of Korea's economic transformation was not so much an ideological tilt toward a large role for government as it was a commitment to policies that empowered state-supported enterprises to take advantage of the international marketplace. The Korean government followed its own brand of trade liberalization, but more importantly, once it decided which path to follow, the government initiated and sustained the measures needed to execute the strategy effectively.

THE STATE OF THE DANCE

Discipline in the context of free trade takes the form of a sustained commitment to easing restrictions on both imports and exports. Yet between November 2008 and November 2010, governments around the world introduced more than 800 new protectionist measures, and there is no apparent slowdown in sight.[18] The G-20 countries, which account for 80 percent of world trade, are the principal source of the problem: they raised 111 discriminatory measures from June 2010 to November 2010 alone. The rise in protectionism belies the pledges made by the G-20 to resist the temptation to erect trade barriers when the global economy took a dive in late 2008. To make matters worse, the G-8, which play a dominant role at the World Bank and the World Trade Organization and are allegedly champions of the free trade agenda, account for almost two-fifths of the discriminatory measures instigated in the past two years.

To a large extent, the tipping point for global trade lies with those developing countries that have not yet had a chance to participate in the dance. Most trade experts agree that some of the largest gains to trade would come from providing farmers in developing countries with undistorted access to potential markets for their agricultural products. But agriculture is one of the areas where the developed world protects its markets most heavily. Among the poorest countries in the world, with a combined average GDP per capita of $637, Benin, Burkina Faso, Chad, and Mali are known as the "Cotton Four" (C-4) because they rely so heavily on the plant for their export revenues. The C-4 produce cotton more cheaply than anywhere else on the planet—an advantage that under truly free global trade would make them prime beneficiaries of the world's ever-increasing desire for everything from bedspreads to baseball caps. The problem is that the United States and the European Union heavily subsidize their own cotton farmers, driving up the global supply of cotton, artificially depressing prices, and undermining the C-4's ability to trade their way out of poverty. Since the launch of the Doha Development Round of trade talks at the WTO, more than $47 billion in subsidies have been doled out to cotton growers, with more than half going directly to US farmers.[19]

Once you strip away the veneer of public pronouncements, the G-8-driven, WTO-facilitated Doha Development Round amounts to "Do as I say, not as I do." Indeed, progress in trade liberalization since 2001 has occurred largely through bilateral and regional trade agreements outside the Doha framework—or through litigation. To get developed countries to dance with them, developing countries have actually had to haul the United States and the European Union into court. For example, in 2002 Brazil filed an official grievance with the WTO against the United States, alleging that its cotton program suppressed global cotton prices and illegally gave the United States higher market share. After two years of litigation, the WTO's dispute settlement panel ruled that the US cotton program did indeed amount to protectionism.

Having pushed developing countries to integrate their national economies with the global marketplace over the past three decades, it is now the rich countries that pose the greatest threat to further progress on free trade. The rise of protectionist sentiment in advanced countries raises important questions for the future of the world economy. Will the World Bank, the WTO, and other international organizations cajole the developed world into reducing barriers to imports—especially agricultural products—with the same gusto they exercised toward developing countries under the auspices of structural adjustment? And will rich-country governments have the courage to pursue the Doha Development Round of trade talks in good faith, despite pressure from domestic interest groups that oppose further liberalization? Nothing less than global prosperity hinges on the answers to these questions.

During tough times such as those now faced in advanced economies, politicians look for scapegoats to blame for stagnant incomes and unemployment. The trade deficit and its alleged cause—imports from China and other developing countries—make easy targets. Leaders who want to do what is best for their countries must tell the truth. We need more not less free trade. With an aging population and mountains of debt, the developed world faces limited domestic demand and resources for years to come. Emerging economies propelled to catch-up growth through free trade have the potential to be a saving grace, buying increased quantities of goods from the developed world.

Although the trade balance is not a causal factor in a country's long-run prosperity, it is a helpful indicator when not being used to score political points. If a country imports more than it exports in a given year, it has a trade deficit. If a country runs trade deficits year after year, it accumulates debt to foreign creditors. A country's annual "current account deficit" equals the trade deficit plus the interest payments on its accumulated stock of debt. The trade and current account deficits are important economic indicators, not because they tell us about the *desirability* of the pattern of a country's resource flows, but because they provide clues about its *sustainability*. At some point, bills must be paid. Large and persistent deficits indicate that a country is rapidly accumulating debt that it will not be able to service if it has not used the borrowed resources wisely (for example, to import capital goods that increase productive capacity). As we will soon see in the next chapter, this issue is distinct from the benefits a country receives from the goods it imports.

CHAPTER 7

CAPITAL AND CAPITOLS

IN POLICYMAKING, AS IN LIFE, DECISIONS DRIVEN BY FEAR and resentment often set in motion a series of self-destructive actions that culminate in precisely the outcome you sought to avoid. In spite of their need for capital in the 1960s and 1970s, Third World countries, afraid of economic domination by the West, resisted foreign ownership of domestic corporations to such an extent that they turned almost exclusively to borrowing from international commercial banks to fund their economic development. In one of the great ironies of recent history, a policy stance intended to protect national sovereignty by keeping the influence of foreign capitalists at bay resulted in a greater loss of agency as developing countries accumulated so much debt that they had to sell iconic national companies to foreign investors at fire-sale prices in order to pay their creditors. Foreign ownership of domestic assets achieved under duress came at a much greater cost to developing countries than if they had let in foreign capital in the first place.

When domestic capital markets function properly, they reallocate savings from households and institutions that have a surplus of resources to investors who have a deficit. Directing savings in this way delivers greater productive efficiency for the economy than we would see if companies and entrepreneurs with great ideas but a shortage of funds had to forgo investment. When opportunity knocks, it's great to have cash on hand, but for those who don't, access to financial markets provides a viable alternative. Capital markets also work well at bringing together savers and investors in an international context—unless, of course, governments refuse to allow the cross-border exchange of financial assets.

INHIBITED INVESTMENT

During the height of the import substitution era, the climate of developing nations turned decidedly cold toward the presence of both foreign investment and savings.[1] Multinational corporations seeking to engage in foreign direct investment (FDI) faced heightened scrutiny from governments that wanted to control the commanding heights of their economies, even if they did not know how to run them properly. In 1969 Kenneth Kaunda, then the president of Zambia, requested that the foreign owners of Zambia's copper mines give 51 percent of their shares to the state. "I do not think," he said, "that the nation can achieve economic independence without acquiring full control of the existing mines."[2] Kaunda's decision to nationalize copper had disastrous consequences. The government tried, in effect, to use the mines as a cash machine to fund projects designed to make the country self-sufficient in manufacturing and other areas. But foreign investment in Zambia declined dramatically in the wake of the country's investor-unfriendly act, and so did its foreign exchange reserves. The government did not have the investment or management skills needed to run the mines, so efficiency plummeted and copper production spiraled downward over the next two decades.[3] Between 1974 and 1994, Zambia's GDP per capita fell by 50 percent, and by the mid-1980s the country had one of the highest ratios of debt to GDP in the world.[4]

Lusaka was not the only capital whose concern about foreign exploitation of the local market caused it to commit significant missteps. Governments that allowed multinationals to repatriate their profits faced the charge that they were allowing foreigners to skim off the wealth created by the hard work of domestic labor. To avoid such criticism, governments went to great lengths to structure deals requiring multinationals to share their technology, management, and marketing skills with local firms—so much so that they often overplayed their hand.

In 1977 India's ruling Janata Party decided to aggressively enforce the country's 1973 Foreign Exchange Regulation Act (FERA) and pushed for partial Indian ownership of all foreign firms operating within the country. IBM decided that it would rather withdraw from the country than comply, and Big Blue was not alone. Coca-Cola, which had reportedly been ready to reach a deal on mixed ownership, pulled out when the Indian government insisted that the company divulge the secret formula for its syrup.[5] Between 1957 and 1973, an average of 568 foreign companies operated in India in any given year. With the more stringent enforcement of the FERA, the average fell to 300 by 1981.[6]

The actions of Zambia and India typified a broader trend toward less-than-welcoming treatment of foreign corporations, which had been on the rise since the 1950s. The trend arguably peaked at a special session of the United Nations General Assembly in May 1974. During that plenary gathering, a group of seventy-seven developing countries known as the G-77 secured a declaration on the establishment of a New International Economic Order (NIEO). Among other things, the NIEO asserted the right of developing countries to exercise control over their natural resources and economic activities, "including the right to nationalization or transfer of ownership to its nationals." By effectively declaring their intention to expropriate multinationals if and when they deemed such action appropriate, developing countries ignored Nelson Rockefeller's observation that "capital likes to go where it is loved" and set a chilling tone toward foreign investment for the rest of the decade.

In accordance with the G-77's increasingly ambivalent relationship with foreign investors, the flow of FDI to the developing world dropped precipitously from its historically high levels. Prior to the G-77's declaration, the ratio of foreign investment to GDP in the developing world had, at times, been as high as 41 percent. By 1980 it had fallen to 24 percent. In Latin America, where the adjective "ambivalent" would be an exceedingly generous characterization of the attitude toward foreign capital, the fall was more acute. By 1980 the ratio of FDI to GDP in Latin America was down to 6 percent from pre-G-77 levels of 56 percent and higher.[7]

With the fall in FDI—much of it occurring in the commanding heights of the economy, where foreign ownership was largely disallowed or expropriated—governments became active participants in a range of key sectors from energy and mining to transportation and hotels, resulting in the buildup of large state-owned enterprises (SOEs). More often than not, state-appointed leadership possessed limited expertise, yet because managers of these institutions could rely on government support, they had little incentive to perform. Instead of receiving FDI and generating profits with the latest equipment, technology, and managerial know-how, the SOEs did not generate growth and often consumed more resources than they produced.

STONEWALLED SAVINGS

While foreign companies did not receive much love at the hands of developing-country governments, the treatment of foreign residents seeking to place their savings in domestic financial instruments was even worse. Governments treated the presence of multinationals in the local economy as a necessary evil, but at least sometimes permitted their existence. Foreign savers were simply blocked. Whether you were an individual who wanted to buy shares on the domestic stock market or a pension fund looking to diversify your clients' equity holdings beyond the borders of Europe, Japan, and North America, the message was largely the same: "Keep out!"

Today, if you want to know how the Jakarta Composite Index is faring, all you have to do is pick up the latest issue of the *Financial Times*. Forty years ago, however, major newspapers did not routinely provide information on emerging stock market valuations. Doing so seemed unnecessary, because the governments of developing countries did not permit foreign nationals to purchase shares of domestic companies. In fact, the term "emerging markets" did not even exist. The rebranding of the "Third World" did not take place until foreigners were allowed to purchase domestic shares in those countries. A key moment occurred during a 1981 meeting at the New York office of Salomon Brothers. Antoine van Agtmael, then an economist at the International Finance Corporation, an arm of the World Bank, tried to pitch a "Third World Equity Fund" to a group of bankers. After somebody in the audience extolled the idea but panned the name, van Agtmael coined the phrase "emerging markets."[8]

Foreigners who wanted to hold their savings in developing-country financial instruments other than stocks found themselves equally frustrated. In most instances, nonresidents could not purchase corporate bonds, certificates of deposit, or commercial paper. In the rare cases where foreigners had the de jure right to hold domestic financial instruments in their portfolios, they were de facto prohibited from doing so by a number of other obstacles. The proclivity of governments for printing money during the 1970s and 1980s virtually wiped out the domestic bond market in many developing countries, since people feared that high inflation would devour the value of their fixed-income portfolios. Local bond markets open to nonresidents were not only unusual but typically too small to accommodate foreign institutional players who had vast pools of savings to allocate and needed deep, liquid markets that could absorb large purchases and sales with a minimal impact on prices.

International commercial banks were the only nonresidents able to circumnavigate the savings stonewall—they could channel their depositors' money to developing-country governments in the form of floating-interest-rate loans. Governments used these loans to fund a wide range of activities, many of which did nothing for the greater good of society. Some loans were wasted outright in conspicuous consumption and white-elephant projects that benefited nobody other than a few venal officials. Other loans were directed at well-intended but largely inefficient investments in state-owned enterprises. There were exceptions, of course, but government activity in the developing world used up a lot of valuable savings—foreign and domestic—without generating significant economic benefits.

FORGONE GROWTH

Whether the issue was savings or investment, portfolio flows or FDI, the bottom line is that the governments of developing countries made it very hard for foreign capital to find its way into the private sector of their domestic economies. Ongoing resistance to foreign capital persisted even as governments were vanquishing inflation and easing restrictions on international trade. It is one thing to tell a country to focus on selling bananas so that its people can buy cars; when foreign car companies come looking to buy the country's banana plantations, however, it is a different matter altogether. Lower inflation and fewer trade restrictions made the local environment a more attractive place to invest. The domestic business community, from large corporations to small-business owners and micro entrepreneurs, naturally wanted to expand. But it is a problem when a large group of people need capital to grow and their only source is limited local savings—scarce resources become dearer yet.

For instance, Tanzania, a country that began liberalizing trade in 1985, still maintains tight controls over nonresident participation in its capital market.[9] Foreigners are limited in their ability to purchase shares and bonds on the national stock exchange, and most inward in-vestments must receive prior approval from the Bank of Tanzania.[10] Tight controls on capital inflows at the macroeconomic level make it exceedingly difficult for individual firms to get the loans they need to grow. In the words of one young Tanzanian entrepreneur, "Our coun-try does not have a system that can enable a person to borrow large amounts of money. That is why you see entrepreneurs like me divide our businesses into several small businesses [in order to gain access to microcredit]."[11]

The experience of the Tanzanian entrepreneur is not unique to Africa. In 1991, as Chile was beginning to rid itself of double-digit inflation, the government imposed "El Encaje," a tax on capital in-flows that lasted from 1991 to 1998. During these seven years, small firms listed on the Chilean stock market suffered tighter financing constraints and reduced their investment even though the economy was experiencing a period of rapid productivity growth.[12]

In a terrible paradox, hard-won reforms such as inflation stabiliza-tion and trade liberalization create a wide range of new private-sector growth opportunities, but a number of them do not go forward owing to a lack of resources. At the same time, a number of old growth op-portunities that would have been implemented in the absence of re-forms—think of the small firms in the previous example of Chile—are pushed aside by the subset of newly created projects that *do* receive funding in a postreform environment.

To see how bad this problem of so-called crowding out can be, re-turn to a measure we looked at earlier, the price-earnings (P/E) ratio, which, you'll recall, is an index of the price per share of the market portfolio divided by an index of earnings. It is a useful indicator be-cause the difference between the P/E ratio of developing-country stock markets and that of the developed world reveals the extent to which growth opportunities in developing countries went unexploited because their governments kept foreign capital out of the country. Ac-cording to Standard & Poor's Emerging Markets Database, the

P/E for Latin American stock markets in 1986 was 3.5 versus 21 for the United States. Flipping the market price-earnings ratio upside down gives us a measure called the "earnings yield" (E/P), which is the average cost of equity capital for a country's publicly traded companies—29 percent in Latin America and 5 percent in the United States in 1986.

These cost-of-capital numbers tell us that in 1986 projects in Latin America needed a prospective return on investment (ROI) in excess of 29 percent to be economically viable, whereas projects in the United States with an ROI of 5 percent or more cleared the bar. For example, a $100 million investment in Latin America expected to make a $28 million profit would have been left on the table while a $100 million investment in the United States with an expected profit of as low as $6 million would have passed muster. If Latin American governments had removed restrictions on nonresident shareholders in 1986, companies in the region would have enjoyed lower borrowing costs and would have been more likely to implement some of those high-return projects left sitting on the table. Similarly, US residents would have benefited from shifting some of their savings from the US equity market to Latin American stocks with higher risk but a higher expected rate of return (we'll talk about risk shortly).

Most businesses in developing and developed countries are not publicly traded and therefore don't raise money for capital projects by floating shares on the stock market. The important point about the earnings yield, however, is that it provides a conservatively low estimate of the cost of capital for the entire economy, because the average cost of borrowing for businesses not listed on the stock market is likely to be greater than or equal to the cost for those that are. If publicly traded corporations in Latin America faced an average cost of capital of 29 percent, then the local dressmaker in Honduras who needed to buy another sewing machine was only able to do so at astronomical rates.[13]

Governments can attempt to circumvent the costs of a closed capital account by spurring domestic savings. Many East Asian countries have done this by instituting mandatory savings accounts; the Central Provident Fund (CPF) in Singapore, for instance, requires workers to contribute as much as 50 percent of their wages.[14] Through vehicles like the CPF, governments in the region have driven up local savings to unprecedented levels and managed to sustain them. Accordingly, in 1986 the average earnings yield in Asian stock markets was 5.4 percent—slightly higher than in the United States, but nowhere near Latin American levels.

But strategies to increase domestic savings entail a significant trade-off: they effectively make poor people consume less so that companies, and in some cases the state, can build factories. During the 1950s, authorities in mainland China and Taiwan required farmers to sell them their agricultural products at below-market prices.[15] This was essentially a policy of forced savings, as it appropriated resources from the household sector (farmers in this case) for the purpose of producing investment goods. This might not sound so bad, but consider that instead of cheaply feeding government workers who were building blast furnaces and other industrial equipment, farming families might have used the money they would have made on an open market to buy shoes for their children.

Policies designed to maintain extremely high levels of savings in emerging economies not only have an important human cost but also fail to address another downside of closed economies. When governments do not permit trade in financial assets, they impose unnecessary volatility on the savings of their citizens. We've already seen the challenges that poor people face in maintaining the value of their savings. Consider now the risk faced by people who hold some of their wealth—the accumulation of past savings—in stocks. Because developing countries contain no shortage of risks, the historical variance of stock returns in emerging economies is several orders of magnitude larger than in developed countries. Bearing all of this risk in isolation is the second factor, in addition to scarcity of capital, that drives up the cost of borrowing for companies in emerging economies.

The good news is that the risks faced by savers in emerging economies are generally not the same as those confronted by savers in the developed world. Stocks in emerging economies tend to do well when stocks in developed countries do badly, and vice versa. This means that residents of rich countries could reduce the overall risk of their equity portfolios by holding some emerging-market stocks. The potential for emerging-market stocks to reduce volatility and increase expected returns for developed-country savers is simply a cross-border manifestation of the relationship between risk and return. Whereas the variance of local stocks determines the risk premium associated with equities in a closed economy, it is the extent to which local stocks spread risk between domestic and foreign residents that drives the premium in a world of open markets. As foreigners buy stocks in liberalizing countries, they spread the risk of these stocks across a greater number of people. Because domestic savers then bear less risk from local stocks, the risk premium falls. International diversification, with the reduction in risk that it brings, has the potential to further reduce the cost of capital for emerging markets.

The bad news is that for decades the potential gains to trade in shares of corporations across international boundaries remained just that—gains to trade in principle only. As domestic stock markets remained closed to foreigners, the opportunities for residents of developed and developing countries to engage in the mutually beneficial spreading of risk across borders were limited to nonexistent. Yet even as governments were resisting flows of portfolio equity and foreign direct investment, the one form of international financial transaction in which they were extensively engaged—borrowing from US and European commercial banks—unwittingly sowed the seeds of greater openness to come.

OPENING UP BY STEPPING DOWN
(FROM THE COMMANDING HEIGHTS)

The late economist Herb Stein said, "If something cannot go on forever, it will stop."[16] The use of bank lending by developing-country authorities to fund their economic ambitions was nothing if not unsustainable. With the help of borrowed money, Third World governments became some of the largest, most diversified—and inefficient—holding companies in the world, driving the commanding heights of their economies off the road to prosperity and into a ditch of red ink.

It was one thing for G-77 officials to keep out portfolio equity and foreign direct investment when American and European bankers were pumping their countries full of liquidity. But it became quite another when the Third World Debt Crisis hit in 1982 and the flow of lending abruptly came to a halt. When countries did not have enough money to pay their creditors and the abyss of financial insolvency loomed large, ideological stances began to give way to more practical considerations. Whether the government retained possession of, say, the national airline became far less important than whether it could find buyers to take loss-making SOEs off its hands and remove an important source of hemorrhaging from the national balance sheet.

But selling off the commanding heights was no simple task. During the process of accumulating massive conglomerates, governments had eaten up years of household and corporate savings without generating much wealth. As a consequence, domestic residents and local businesses did not have the capacity to purchase all of the SOEs that governments needed to offload. To divest the billions of dollars' worth of assets they had accumulated over the years, states needed outside help to grease the wheels of privatization. *Time* magazine aptly captured the tenor of the change in 1991:

Get a great deal on a Mexican phone company! Pick up a
Philippine airline—cheap! Like shopkeepers clearing out su-
perfluous inventory, governments around the world are
dumping a vast array of state-owned assets onto the open
market. . . . For finance ministers from Brasilia to Budapest,
the disposal of publicly owned enterprises has become the
great hope for debt-burdened economies. The offerings include huge industrial conglomerates and small retail chains,
banks and restaurants, oil fields, utilities and hotels.[17]

Out of necessity more than anything else, developing-country governments began opening their stock markets to nonresident savers in
the late 1980s and early 1990s.[18] A few countries lifted virtually all restrictions overnight, but most proceeded more gradually. Nevertheless, the extent of the change was soon undeniable. In 1984 the
number of developing nations that permitted foreigners to purchase
shares could be counted on one hand. By 1994, there were at least
twenty countries in which nonresidents could buy stocks through a
variety of savings vehicles ranging from closed-end country funds,
which are mutual funds that specialize in the stocks of a given country, to American depositary receipts (ADRs), the term for shares of
non-US companies that trade on US stock exchanges. As the legal
barriers to the purchase of domestic equity by foreign nationals declined, nonresidents plowed their savings into the now "emerging
markets" to buy shares of newly privatized companies, seeking to take
advantage of opportunities to earn higher expected rates of return on
capital and diversify risk. Inflows of equity capital to developing countries, which had been practically nonexistent in 1970, soared to
US$100 billion by 1994.

It is important to note that stock market liberalization facilitated a
great deal of foreign direct investment by transferring company control rights to nonresidents. Thinking about FDI typically brings
"greenfield" investments to mind—for example, Intel building a plant

from scratch in Costa Rica—but FDI also occurs whenever a nonresident purchases 10 percent or more of the voting shares of a preexisting but newly privatized local company.[19] Between 1991 and 2000, 48 percent of FDI in Latin America and 61 percent in Asia occurred through the transfer of shares.[20]

As countries removed barriers to portfolio flows and ownership rights, savings became more abundant and risk-sharing increased between domestic and foreign shareholders, reducing the cost of capital and driving up stock prices. Controlling as always for a variety of potentially confounding factors, including the simultaneous occurrence of other economic reforms, the average emerging economy's stock market experienced cumulative abnormal returns of 40 percent in anticipation of opening up.[21] To be precise, the revaluation of local stocks occurred in the twelve-month period *preceding* the implementation of stock market liberalizations. As in earlier chapters, it is important to ask whether a pre-event window conveys the full impact of this policy change.

If foreign savers had been skeptical that governments would remain committed to open capital markets, then they initially might have thought that there was a high probability that local authorities would reverse their decision to liberalize. In the presence of this kind of uncertainty, abnormal returns computed over a twelve-month pre-event window would understate the true impact of liberalization. Only as governments stayed the course and nonresident savers became convinced that open capital markets were here to stay would stock prices fully incorporate the benefits of opening up.

Adjusting the event window to account for the gradual buildup of credibility reveals stunning facts. Emerging economies experienced cumulative abnormal returns on the order of 50 percent in the first year following the month in which liberalizations were implemented, and an additional 25 percent over the course of the next two years.[22] Tallying up these cumulative abnormal returns (75 percent) and adding them to the 40 percent figure from the year prior to liberalization, we see that opening the stock market to nonresident savers produced cumulative abnormal returns on the order of 115 percent over a four-year period.

Higher stock prices in emerging economies immediately made at least three groups of people very happy: Domestic residents who sold shares to foreigners realized large capital gains. Domestic residents who did not sell their stocks also become wealthier because the value of their portfolios increased. And all foreign buyers gained more diversified portfolios; indeed, some, depending on the timing of their entry into the market, may also have experienced capital gains.

It is perhaps not surprising that shareholders benefited from a policy change that gave them more options for holding their savings and diversifying risk, but what about the vast majority of people in emerging economies who did not (or could not) own stocks? What benefits, if any, did they reap from liberalization? The answer, it turns out, is: quite a bit.

Prosperous Portfolios
and Winning Wages

Millions of people in the developing world who never owned shares, much less understood the finer points of the price-earnings ratio, benefited substantially from stock market liberalization. By driving up investment, productivity, and wages, the opening of capital markets delivered greater material prosperity for legions of workers in emerging economies, irrespective of whether they had personal stock portfolios.

As the cost of financing fell in liberalizing economies, many capital projects that had not been viable before opening up became profitable. With increased incentive to expand and an influx of foreign savings to finance their plans, local companies ramped up investment. In a sample of eighteen emerging economies in Africa, Asia, and Latin

America that liberalized between 1986 and 1995, the growth rate of the capital stock increased from an average of 5.4 percentage points per year in the five-year period preceding liberalization to 6.5 percentage points per year in the subsequent five.[23]

The impact of investment on productivity and wages follows immediately from our discussion of the determinants of gross domestic product—capital, labor, and ideas. As firms increased investment, workers across the emerging world had more and better machines with which to do their jobs. Not surprisingly, then, the same sample of eighteen countries that increased investment following liberalization also experienced a surge in productivity. The growth rate of output per worker rose from an average of 1.4 percent per year in the five years prior to opening to an average of 3.7 percent per year in the postliberalization period.

But this 2.3-percentage-point increase in productivity growth experienced by liberalizing countries is too large to be explained purely by the 1.1-percentage-point increase in the growth rate of their capital stocks. Because there are only three factors of production, the inability of capital alone to explain the increase in labor productivity points to the important role of ideas. Much of the productivity increase was likely to have been the consequence of new technology and managerial know-how—foreign partners, supply chain connections, and access to new markets—that came with the FDI facilitated by the lifting of restrictions on share ownership.

Greater productivity made firms more profitable—that is one reason why stock prices increased—but wages rose as well. Yet another study of liberalizing countries found that, during the first three years after opening to foreign capital, the typical worker in the manufacturing sector saw her real wages rise seven times faster than would otherwise have been the case.[24] Put in monetary terms, the average worker's total compensation increased by about US$487—nearly a 20 percent increase in take-home pay that would not have occurred in the absence of liberalization.

The impact of capital account liberalization on growth took the economics profession by surprise. For years scholars had searched for a connection between capital account policy and economic growth using the same flawed methodology they employed to try to connect trade liberalization and growth. Economists had been asking whether countries with open capital markets grew faster than countries with closed capital markets, when instead they should have asked whether the countries that liberalized their stock markets experienced faster growth than they would have otherwise.[25]

RECIPROCITY, NOT RESISTANCE

Fear and resentment have no place in a disciplined approach to economic policy. Neither a nation's people nor their government needs complete ownership or control of the corporations operating inside their borders to reap substantial benefits from their presence. In a similar vein, foreigners need not take controlling stakes in domestic companies in order to benefit from the local capital market. There is an important lesson of reciprocity here. When governments permit nonresident ownership of portfolio equity, domestic residents share the risk of local stocks with foreign nationals. Foreigners are willing to bear the risk because emerging-market equities give them a claim to the expected future profits of companies doing business in a rapidly growing economy.

In the 1970s, their fear of foreign domination led developing-country governments to strong-arm multinational corporations in an attempt to force them to give over their secrets to making everything from soft drinks to semiconductors. But countries do not need to possess the secrets of multinationals in order to benefit from their investments. FDI plays a central role in economic development by allowing nations to play leapfrog with the innovation process. Instead of trying to develop ideas from scratch—a process that can take decades—countries can permit foreign corporations to bring in new technology and managerial know-how that drives up productivity.

When all is said and done, the liberalization of portfolio equity and foreign direct investment increases prosperity for both foreign and domestic residents. For domestic corporations, the cost of capital falls, leading to more investment, faster growth, and higher wages for their workers. Having taken the necessary steps to stabilize the domestic economy and harness the power of free trade and private enterprise, leaders who grant access to capital and enable risk-sharing across borders can help ensure that the opportunities created do not become dreams deferred.

As we shall soon see, however, not all international capital flows are created equal. Too much debt and not enough equity can catapult economies into crisis. And to understand how a crisis can be resolved efficiently—whether in an advanced country or a developing country—we need to understand what discipline means in the context of creditors and debtors.

CHAPTER 8

CRISES AND THE
DEBT DISTINCTION

HAVING SHED THEIR "THIRD WORLD" MONIKER IN FAVOR OF the more fashionable title "emerging markets," developing countries in the 1990s became increasingly attractive destinations for foreign money. With their stock exchanges finally accessible to the outside world, significant quantities of equity capital began flowing to emerging economies. And as good times began to roll, suppliers of capital operating in the parallel world of debt paid very close attention.

At first, the nascent asset class of emerging-market bonds seemingly provided just the right instrument to align the desires of foreign savers with the financing needs of governments in the developing world. Eager to complement the action on the equity side, financial institutions tasked with allocating billions of dollars of household savings parked in pension and mutual funds stuffed their portfolios with emerging-market government bonds. Finance ministries in the emerging world were equally complicit. Giddy, perhaps, with their newfound freedom to sidestep commercial banks—a freedom that provided external validation of a decade's worth of difficult internal reforms—they gorged on the proceeds of these bond sales to the developed world.

But loans are loans, regardless of whether they come from banks or bondholders. And so it was that even as they moved to greater quantities of equity financing, developing countries embarked on yet another path of inadvisably heavy borrowing, having failed to learn the general lesson of their experience in the 1980s. Financing economic development with ever-increasing amounts of debt is an invitation to hardship. Doing it by issuing short-term, dollar-denominated bonds to a far-flung group of individuals who had no mechanism or incentive to cooperate in times of distress was, in colloquial American parlance, a double dog dare.

Mexico, the nation that triggered the Third World Debt Crisis with its default in 1982, was again the first country to get into trouble. In January 1994, the country's central bank had more than US$30 billion of reserves. By Christmas, less than US$5 billion remained. When Mexican authorities offered to sell the market an additional US$600 million worth of *Tesobonos,* short-term dollar-denominated Mexican bonds, but received bids for only US$28 million, they were forced to devalue the currency to avoid running out of reserves. In only a few months, the peso lost more than half its value against the US dollar. Because many Mexican businesses had also borrowed in dollars, the free fall of the peso made it more expensive to service their debts. A full-blown domestic banking crisis ensued as local financial institutions suddenly found themselves stuck with a mountain of nonperforming loans. With the country sliding toward the abyss, owners of Mexican securities of all kinds (not just Tesobonos) made a beeline for the exit. Interest rates and risk premia soared, the stock market plunged, GDP fell by 6.2 percent—one of the worst contractions on record—and over half a million workers lost their jobs.[1]

The Mexican crisis turned out to be just the beginning. In 1997 financial turmoil found its way to Asian shores, beginning first with Thailand, then hitting South Korea, Indonesia, and Malaysia before heading west to Russia in 1998 and Brazil in 1999.[2] Argentina's epic default in 2001 made the Mexican crisis look like child's play.

The experiences of Latin America and Asia in the mid- to late 1990s illustrate the dark side of international capital flows. Following the string of financial crises in emerging economies, capital account liberalization came under fierce attack. Although liberalization brought a lower cost of capital, greater investment, faster growth, and higher wages to the emerging world, professors and policymakers who supported the reform were forced to confront the criticisms that went along with the decision to admit foreign savings and investment. Letting in foreign capital invited speculative movements of "hot" money that flowed into the country upon opening but rushed for the exit at the first sign of trouble, wreaking havoc on the stability of developing economies.[3] Superficially, the collapse in asset prices, output, and investment in Latin America and Asia suggests that capital account liberalizations cause crises and that the efficiency benefits of opening up simply do not outweigh the costs.

But discipline demands distinctions. It makes no sense to embrace the conclusion that "liberalizations cause crises" without specifying what kind of liberalizations. In its broadest form, a capital account liberalization is any decision by a government that allows capital to flow more freely into or out of the country. We can divide the types of liberalization into two categories: those involving debt, such as bank loans and bonds, and those that involve equity, such as ordinary shares of company stock. It turns out that this distinction provides the clarity we need to zero in on the kinds of liberalizations that succeed—and the kinds that fail. Debt played a central role in every major emerging-market financial crisis of the past quarter-century. Debt also triggered the financial crisis that ravaged the United States, the United Kingdom, and other industrialized nations in 2008–2009. None of these crises *originated* in the stock market.

Debt Versus Equity

The distinction between debt and equity turns on the difference between liability and risk-sharing. A debt contract such as a bank loan or bond requires regular payments to the lender, regardless of the borrower's financial circumstances. In contrast, an equity contract involves risk-sharing—large payouts for shareholders when times are good and little to nothing when times are bad. Because debt contracts do not embody risk-sharing, too much debt makes countries vulnerable to financial distress when their economic fortunes change suddenly. For instance, when bad news arrives about a country's ability to service its debt, such as a fall in the price of its major export, lenders will rush to get their money while there is still money to be had.

It may seem as though foreign equity financing makes countries just as susceptible to crises as debt financing, but foreign purchases of domestic stocks cannot simply be reversed if foreign shareholders become skittish about a nation's prospects. Shareholders who want their money back have to sell their stocks to a willing buyer, and prices will drop as soon as other market participants (domestic or foreign) anticipate the increase in the supply of shares. As stock prices fall, so does the incentive to sell. Furthermore, whereas panic-filled creditors tend to make debt service payments go up when a country is in trouble, exacerbating the crisis, equity financing gives the option of paying out less cash to shareholders, thereby helping to stabilize foreign reserves.

Make no mistake, stock prices drop when financial crises occur, but stock markets are not the cause of the problem. The fall in prices simply reflects the changing economic reality. Financial crises increase required rates of return by driving up interest rates and risk premia; they also reduce expected future cash flows by plunging the economy into recession and decimating earnings. The decline in equity prices may also exacerbate financial crises through important side effects. For example, when stock prices fall, people lose wealth, become more anxious about the future, and cut back on purchases of everything from washing machines to flat-screen televisions. The drop in consumption hurts sales and prompts stores to lay off workers. Unemployed workers consume less, further reducing demand and creating a downward economic spiral. But the truth is that the stock market would reflect and transmit the impact of financial crises in this manner even if it were closed to foreign investment. In fact, opening up may actually ameliorate the impact of crises by creating a more liquid equity market through which a larger pool of potential investors can purchase distressed assets.

Returning to the problem of debt, it is reasonable to ask why debt, if it is so dangerous, is so prevalent. A large part of the answer lies in the rules of the international financial system. Economist Jeremy Bulow argues that the Foreign Sovereign Immunities Act of 1976 in the United States and the State Immunities Act of 1978 in the United Kingdom have effectively moved the jurisdiction over sovereign commercial transactions (for example, selling bonds) to First World courts. As a result, developed-country entities that purchase emerging-market government debt in the United States or the United Kingdom can resort to the courts of those countries in the event of a payment dispute. No such avenue of recourse exists for purchasers of emerging-market equity.[4] Because international law, however unwittingly, protects the rights of debt holders more vigilantly than those of equity holders, it is not surprising that suppliers of capital to emerging markets lean heavily toward debt. Weak local protection of shareholders' rights and a lack of transparency in developing-country stock markets reinforce the tendency of developed-country savers to supply debt to emerging markets instead of equity.[5] Biases in international banking regulations lead to other unintended consequences as well. For instance, the Basel Capital Accord of 1988 introduced a risk-adjusted weighting system for loans that regulators thought would increase the safety of banks. Instead, the new regulations inadvertently drove lending to emerging markets in the 1990s toward the most dangerous form of debt—short-term liabilities that are due in three months and must be paid in dollars.[6]

LIQUIDITY VERSUS SOLVENCY

As important as distinctions are for the diagnosis of crises, they are even more central to constructing a cure. What you do to resolve a financial crisis depends on whether the crisis stems from a problem of illiquidity or insolvency. Illiquidity is simply the cash flow shortage that most families face from time to time. We all know the sinking feeling that sets in when a stack of bills (rent, telephone, credit card, utilities, and so on) shows up before the paycheck arrives. The money is on the way, but there are consequences if we can't pay our bills on time. A country's government faces the same problem—albeit on a much larger scale—if frightened creditors demand repayment when its foreign exchange reserves are low and it cannot find new lenders.

Because liquidity problems curtail access to credit and drive up interest rates, they produce spectacular falls in asset prices, output, and employment. As financial institutions and other custodians of savings grow increasingly unwilling to buy a government's debt, the private sector faces a difficult time securing the loans it needs for ongoing investment; as a result, projects must be placed on hold and growth slows down. But swift, decisive, and overwhelming financial support for a government caught in a liquidity bind will ease its cash flow problems, restore its creditworthiness, and put its country on the road to recovery (provided that the government also does its part). For example, when faced with its liquidity crisis in December 1994, Mexico sought financial assistance from the International Monetary Fund and received an emergency loan package in fairly short order. Although a deep recession ensued in 1995, Mexico bounced back quickly, growing by 5.1 percent in 1996 and 6.8 percent the following year.

The extension of emergency funds to help Mexico avert default was not an IMF-only affair. US president Bill Clinton decided to bolster the IMF's US$18 million loan package with US$20 billion from the Treasury's Exchange Stabilization Fund. This move caused a political firestorm in the US Congress, but the United States was not the only country to "top up" the IMF's loan. Mexico also received US$10 billion from the Bank for International Settlements and US$2 billion from the Bank of Canada, for a total in international financial assistance of a then-record-setting US$50 billion.

Today it is still not unusual for a consortium of sovereign lenders such as the European Union to contribute to the IMF's lending efforts in an attempt to prevent contagion—the spread of a debt crisis in one nation to other countries that previously appeared to have sound finances. Contagion is a kind of guilt by association. When the market learned in 1997 that Thailand did not have sufficient foreign exchange reserves to service its short-term debt, lenders with exposure to Thailand tightened their credit standards and attempted to raise the extra capital they needed to offset the losses they expected to suffer on their Thai holdings. But as one set of lenders moved to reduce their credit exposure and raise capital, others observed this behavior and attempted to do likewise. Before long, everybody wanted to pull out of not just Thailand but South Korea, Malaysia, and Indonesia as well. No private creditors were willing to lend at all, and the financial crisis spread through emerging markets more generally.

If a liquidity crisis is what occurs when your bills show up before your paycheck arrives, an insolvency crisis is what happens when your paycheck is not big enough to cover your bills. In contrast to problems of liquidity, access to new loans cannot resolve crises of solvency. If a family will not earn enough money to pay all of its bills, no matter how much time it is given, then extending another loan simply pulls the family into ever-greater indebtedness.

Overhang and Underinvestment

A country suffers from insolvency and what is known as "debt over-hang" if it owes more money to its creditors than it can pay.[7] The advanced economies of Greece, Italy, and Spain are the most recent additions to the debt overhang club. Because people who want to make profits do not lend to governments that cannot return the money with interest, a country saddled with overhang cannot attract new funds on its own. This simple fact has important consequences for a country's investment and growth.

A government that is unable to borrow and does not wish to stoke inflation by printing money must raise taxes to service its debt. This means that debt overhang increases the private sector's expected future tax bill, diverts the benefits of new investment from the private sector to holders of government debt, and reduces the incentive to invest in productive activity. As a result, companies in a country suffering from debt overhang will forgo many profitable new projects. Why invest if all the profits will go to holders of government paper?

Debt overhang is a problem for lenders as well as for the country. As investment falls, growth decreases and government revenues decline, exacerbating the debt-servicing predicament. With slow economic growth (if not outright contraction) and a rising risk of default, the market value of the country's debt begins to fall. The perverse combination of falling growth and falling market values harms both the country and its bondholders. So what is to be done about it? A generation of economists has tackled this question, producing two basic schools of thought: those who think that creditors should take a stiff dose of reality and give debt relief to the country in question, and those who argue that debt relief will only amplify the debtor's problems.

Debt-relief advocates argue that lenders must acknowledge their collective mistake of having extended too much credit, recognize that the face value of the debt overstates its market worth, and write it down to levels that the country could be reasonably expected to service. If each creditor agreed to forgive some of its claims, then the debtor would be better able to service its total debt and the expected value of all creditors' loan portfolios would increase. This is easier said than done, however. First, there is a coordination problem. The creditors must be brought to the negotiation table. This was not inordinately hard to do during the Third World Debt Crisis, when the creditors primarily consisted of New York banks whose CEOs could be summoned by Secretary of State James Baker and Fed chairman Paul Volcker to a meeting in Washington. Getting the right people to the table became much harder following the advent of emerging-market bonds, when developing-country creditors became a heterogeneous group of bondholders spread all over the globe. Second, any individual creditor would naturally prefer the "free ride" of maintaining the full value of its claims while letting the others write off some of their debt. A third party with deep pockets, like the IMF, can help solve the free-rider problem by refusing to provide short-term liquidity until all creditors explicitly acknowledge the long-term solvency problem of the borrower and accept losses on their loan portfolios—called taking a "haircut" in the argot of international finance.

The lender of last resort also plays an important role by ensuring that debt relief is no walk in the park for the recipient of forgiveness. Having taken on more debt than it could afford, the country must agree to change its ways and adopt tough measures—the kinds of reforms discussed in previous chapters—to ensure that it can service the new level of debt and avoid falling into future payment difficulties. Provided that the country sticks to its reform program, debt relief boosts the incentive to undertake profitable investments that have the potential to increase expected future growth rates, cash flows, and the country's debt-servicing capability. In short, debt-relief advocates argue that both borrowers and lenders will benefit from debt forgiveness when a country suffers from debt overhang.

Skeptics say that the arguments in favor of debt forgiveness ignore its potential risks, pointing out at least three adverse effects of debt relief on the recipient country: First, by easing budget constraints, debt relief permits governments to prolong wasteful economic policies that inhibit economic growth. Second, countries that do not honor their debts often incur the wrath of the international community in the form of sanctions that reduce their access to trade.[8] Third, forgiveness involves the restructuring of debt—a breach of contract that may damage the debtor's reputation for repayment and raise its future cost of borrowing in international capital markets.

DEBT FORGIVENESS: DIVINE OR DEBILITATING?

Do the benefits of debt forgiveness outweigh the potential costs, or is it just a harmful policy intervention? With advocates and critics offering legitimate theoretical arguments about the pros and cons of debt relief, the best way to resolve the issue is to look at what actually transpired as developing countries wrestled with the overhang of debt they accumulated during the ill-advised lending boom of the 1970s. The accumulation of liabilities and the crisis that it triggered became a major item on the agenda of the US Treasury for the duration of the 1980s.

During the Third World Debt Crisis, the US Treasury took two distinct approaches to resolve the problem of debt overhang. First, you will recall, was the Baker Plan, which called for reforms and encouraged new lending but provided no debt relief whatsoever. Reforms generated substantial economic value for countries that took them seriously. But we also know that reforms alone were not enough to resolve the problem, because the debt crisis was still a major issue when Nicholas Brady succeeded Baker as secretary of the Treasury in 1988.

Under Brady's leadership, the United States spearheaded a plan that brought sixteen developing countries to debt-relief agreements. Eleven of these countries were in Latin America: Argentina, Bolivia, Brazil, Costa Rica, the Dominican Republic, Ecuador, Mexico, Panama, Peru, Uruguay, and Venezuela. The other five were Bulgaria, Jordan, Nigeria, the Philippines, and Poland. Starting with Mexico in 1989, governments announced and signed Brady deals as they came to agreements with their creditors. The restructuring details differed from country to country, but the central point is that the Brady Plan reduced interest payments or forgave principal and lengthened the maturities of the loans.[9] The plan restructured both commercial bank loans to the central government and loans that the central government had guaranteed on behalf of others: trade credit, project finance, and bank loans to regional governments and state-owned enterprises. All in all, the Brady Plan restructured approximately US$202.8 billion worth of debt, resulting in US$64.7 billion of debt forgiveness. In return, the sixteen "Brady countries" agreed to deepen their commitment to the very policies that many critics of reform would later claim had been the source of their economic problems in the first place: stabilization, liberalization, and privatization.

If the expected future costs of debt-relief agreements outweighed the benefits, then stock prices should have fallen in countries that made the announcements. That was not the case. In anticipation of the official announcement of its Brady deal, the average country's stock market experienced cumulative abnormal returns of 60 percent over the twelve-month pre-announcement period. Importantly, the stock market gains from debt relief did not simply reflect a transfer of wealth to the debtor nations from international commercial banks. The stocks of the eleven major US commercial banks with large developing-country loan exposure also experienced positive cumulative abnormal returns—35 percent over the relevant twelve-month pre-announcement window.[10]

The removal of debt overhang produced more than higher stock prices. Investment surged in the Brady countries after they received debt forgiveness. The average annual growth rate of their capital stocks increased from 1.6 percent per year in the five years prior to debt relief to 3.5 percent per year in the subsequent five.[11] The higher rate of investment in combination with greater total factor productivity (induced by the accompanying reforms) drove up the average growth rate of GDP per capita in the Brady countries over the same time period, from an average of zero to 1.6 percent per year.

Stock prices, investment, and GDP rose because of the direct and indirect effects of debt forgiveness and policy reform. The direct effect was that the Brady Plan led to the forgiveness of approximately US$65 billion of debt. This number is large in absolute terms but small in comparison to the indirect effect of debt forgiveness—the US$210 billion of cumulative net capital inflows (much of it equity) that the Brady countries received in the five-year period following official settlement with their creditors. By eliminating overhang, debt forgiveness created incentives for companies to invest.

While forgiveness provided an important carrot for the private sector in middle-income developing countries stricken by the Third World Debt Crisis, let's not forget the pivotal role of sticks. Implementation of, and sustained commitment to, economic reforms by governments was an essential part of Secretary Brady's strategy for stimulating growth through the elimination of debt overhang. The three nations that failed to sustain reforms—Jordan, Nigeria, and the Philippines—experienced a smaller initial rise in the value of their stock markets than the other Brady countries—30 percent versus 60 percent. Furthermore, even those more modest increases completely evaporated within a year as the lack of commitment to reforms became clear (see Figure 8.1).

This is not to say that life after debt relief was smooth sailing for countries that pursued reforms with greater diligence. The stock market tells us that loan forgiveness and economic reforms were expected

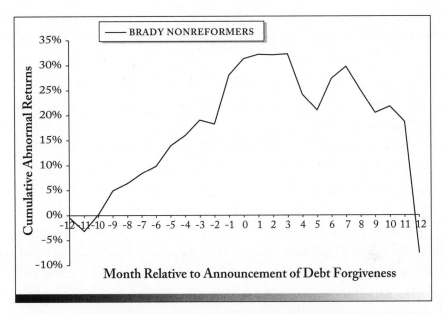

to produce efficient resolutions to the problem of debt overhang, but we know from the opening to this chapter that carelessness with debt got many of these same countries into liquidity problems just a few years after the Brady Plan resolved their solvency issues. In fact, even nations like Korea that managed to steer clear of major debt difficulties in the 1980s and therefore had no need to participate in the Brady Plan fell victim to the perils of debt in the 1990s. The need for vigilance is ever-present—and not just in emerging economies.

RELIEF AND REFORM

Financial crises are spectacular events, ostensible signs of the evils of globalization writ large. When crises hit, they disrupt societies and weaken popular support for changes that have the power to raise long-run living standards. Yet the evidence suggests that globalization—worldwide trade in goods and capital—is the surest means of raising living standards over long periods of time. Capital account opening can bring many benefits, but countries need to proceed with caution because international financial flows are biased toward debt over equity.

When a country's liabilities accumulate beyond a manageable threshold and debt overhang sets in, borrowers *and* lenders are to blame. Both must shoulder the burden of finding an efficient solution. Reforms for indebted nations are critical, but lenders have to do their part too. It makes no difference whether we are talking about Portugal or Peru—when liabilities become so large as to be counterproductive, lenders must write off loans so that countries can reform, grow, and service the more manageable debt burden that remains after lenders have taken their "haircuts."

Although serious debt issues will remain on the table in developed economies for many years to come, it is still far from clear whether advanced nations have the political will to undertake the reforms needed to bring their own debts under control and raise productivity. At present, Europe and the United States appear to have a peculiar aversion to taking the stabilization and structural-adjustment medicine they've been prescribing to developing nations for years with the help of the IMF and the World Bank.

The good news is that the principles—if not the details—of what needs to happen are evident from the lessons of past debt crises in emerging economies. Just as reducing fiscal deficits played a central role in making debt relief a useful part of developing-country growth strategies, the US government needs to undertake some combination of spending cuts and tax increases. Uncle Sam does not need debt relief, and reasonable people can disagree about the extent to which the government should focus on spending or taxes en route to fiscal sustainability, but the basic prescription is the same. In Europe, where the problems increasingly look to be ones of insolvency and overhang, forgiveness and restructuring of debt will have to be one side of the solution. The other side? Structural reform of troubled economies, which could include everything from changes to the collective bargaining processes that have systematically driven up wages faster than productivity to easing restrictions on hiring and firing so that firms will be more enthusiastic about employing new workers.

Attaining higher levels of productivity is the only reliable way for countries such as Greece and Spain to generate the resources required to service their debts—even at reduced levels—and provide for their aging populations. The precise recipe will differ from country to country, but the common denominator must be a persistent devotion to policies that deliver a higher average standard of living. Debt relief has an important role to play in resolving problems of insolvency. But when you have gotten into trouble by borrowing too much money, there is no substitute for learning to live within your means while you increase your capacity to generate future earnings.

CHAPTER 9

THE DEBT-RELIEF
DETOUR

IN THE WORLD'S POOREST COUNTRIES, ONE IN TEN INFANTS die at birth. For those who survive, life is an uphill battle. The three-headed scourge of malaria, HIV/AIDS, and malnutrition conspire to deliver a life expectancy of around forty-two years in places like Mozambique, where the average individual will be approaching her deathbed just as her counterparts in the United States enter middle age and the prime income-earning years of their lives.[1] Numbers such as these are hard to take, and people find talk of death and destitution unpleasant. Something must be to blame, and during the last decade of the twentieth century, the debt of the world's poorest countries provided a highly visible target for men and women of noble intentions.

As the result of growing public sentiment that debt posed the greatest obstacle to improving living standards for the most impoverished places on earth, in 1996 the World Bank and the International Monetary Fund launched the Heavily Indebted Poor Country (HIPC) Initiative, which created a process and timetable for debt forgiveness for nations with high levels of debt and annual GDP per capita of less than US$695. The HIPC Initiative required countries to show a track record of reform in the areas of macroeconomic stabilization and structural adjustment for three years before they reached a "completion point" and received debt relief. In principle, requiring a track record was a good idea. But only six of the countries that tried—Bolivia, Burkina Faso, Guyana, Mali, Mozambique, and Uganda—reached their completion points under the original HIPC framework, and a consensus emerged that poor countries needed "faster, broader, and deeper debt relief."[2]

The global chattering class, wracked with angst about the plight of the poor, publicly lamented the inadequacies of the HIPC framework. Pontiffs, pop stars, and politicians joined forces to push for deeper debt relief delivered at a faster pace. In 1998 Pope John Paul II issued a papal bull calling on wealthy countries to relieve the debts of developing nations in order to "remove the shadow of death" under which they lived.[3] At a June 1999 meeting of G-8 leaders in Cologne, Germany, Bono, lead singer of the rock band U2, presented Chancellor Gerhard Schroeder with 17 million signatures in support of a new effort, the Jubilee 2000 Debt Relief Initiative.[4] Slowly but surely, momentum began to build. In response to the rising tide of pressure, heads of state at the July 2005 G-8 summit at Gleneagles in Scotland called on the IMF, the World Bank, and the African Development Bank to cancel 100 percent of their debt claims on the world's poorest countries. In a rare moment of international consensus, all three institutions assented, giving birth to the Multilateral Debt Relief Initiative (MDRI) and a burst of optimism for the plight of the bottom billion.

Today many people still view the MDRI as a major step in the direction of helping poor countries accomplish the United Nations Millennium Development Goals—tasks such as eradicating extreme poverty and hunger by 2015, achieving universal primary education, reducing infant mortality, and combating HIV/AIDS, malaria, and other diseases. The positive impact of debt relief on stock prices, investment, and economic growth in the poor-but-not-destitute Brady countries tempts one to conclude that it would be even more beneficial to the most indigent nations of the world—places like Benin, Burundi, and Burkina Faso. After all, if debt relief helped the economies of nations with average annual incomes of US$5,000 per capita, wouldn't it accomplish even more good in places where people live on little more than a dollar a day? The reality, surprisingly, provides little support for this conclusion.

MISSING MARKETS

When I began conducting the research that went into this chapter, I hoped to apply the tools of my trade to strengthen the case for debt forgiveness. In particular, I was eager to extend the stock market analysis of the Brady Plan to the context of the HIPCs, and I set about collecting the data required to do so.

There was just one problem. Every attempt I made to locate the necessary information ran into a dead end. The usual source of developing-country equity prices, Standard & Poor's Emerging Markets Database, did not contain information on stock markets in countries such as Rwanda and Niger. Searching libraries, trawling the Web, and placing dozens of phone calls also failed to uncover any data that would be useful for a systematic study. Even Global Financial Data, an online company that provides a treasure trove of arcane historical data not readily available elsewhere, did not have information on HIPC stock prices.

Because the world's poorest countries either did not publish reliable stock market data or lacked public equity markets altogether, it simply was not possible to use local stock price data to measure people's expectations about the future impact of debt relief on HIPC economies. Also, in contrast to the study of the Brady Plan countries, it was not possible to look at the impact of debt relief on the stock prices of the institutions to whom the HIPCs owed money. The establishments that lent money to the HIPCs were not publicly traded financial institutions like the commercial banks that lent money to the Brady countries in the 1970s. Instead, they were sovereign nations and multilateral lending agencies like the IMF, the World Bank, and the

African Development Bank—institutions for which there are no stock prices.

The absence of stock market data with which to assess past HIPC debt-relief efforts forced me to reconsider my quest. Equity markets played a central role in the recovery of the Brady countries post debt relief. Rising stock prices signaled to domestic and international investors that debt relief had removed debt overhang, returned solvency, and restored the profitability of future private-sector projects. Furthermore, the stock market served as a conduit for much of the capital that helped fund those projects, facilitating foreign direct investment and the transfer of new technology and providing a mechanism through which governments privatized billions of dollars of state-owned enterprises. Because stock markets played a fundamental role in the diagnosis and resolution of debt problems in Latin America, their virtual nonexistence in the HIPCs suggested that the debt overhang framework might not be relevant for these countries. But how could I seriously suggest that indigent nations owing billions of dollars to pinstriped bankers did not have a debt problem?[5] Turning from a fruitless search for HIPC stock prices to the data that *did* exist helped answer the question.

If debt overhang had been a problem for the HIPCs, then, like the Brady countries during the 1980s Third World Debt Crisis, they should have experienced net capital outflows as creditors rushed to collect their money and their debt-service payments exceeded the amount of new money coming in. This did not happen to the HIPCs at the height of the Jubilee 2000 Debt Relief Initiative, nor has it ever been the case. Between 2000 and 2005, capital inflows to the HIPCs were roughly 15 percent of GDP—much larger than capital outflows, which averaged roughly 3 percent of GDP. Looking at an even broader span of time, the world's poorest countries have received positive net capital inflows dating back to 1970.[6] If debt relief works by restoring capital flows in places where they have dried up, then the

means by which it would help a set of countries in the midst of a de-
cades-long stream of uninterrupted positive net resource flows is far
from clear.

INCENTIVES, NOT OVERHANG

To use a medical analogy, the Brady countries and the HIPCs were
and are different patients with different illnesses. The treatment that
worked for the former is not relevant for the latter. Debt relief is unlikely to help the HIPCs because, unlike the middle-income Brady
countries, their main economic difficulty is not debt overhang but the
absence of a functional economic system that provides the necessary
incentives for investment and growth. Counterintuitively, debt relief is
more efficient for Brady-like middle-income countries than for low-
income ones, because of how it leverages the private sector. The Brady
countries had functional (if underperforming) economies, viable private sectors, and potential investments of interest to foreign capital.
The low-income HIPCs do not.

One indication that a country's private sector has profitable projects
is that the country attracts private capital flows. The Brady countries
and the HIPCs show stark differences on this score. As early as 1974,
capital flows to the Brady countries' private sectors (private debt, foreign direct investment, and portfolio equity) comprised nearly half of
their net capital inflows. By 1994 the private sector was the destination for the majority of capital flows to the Brady nations.[7] In contrast, the HIPCs' private sectors never attracted significant resources.
More than 90 percent of capital inflows to the world's poorest nations
have taken the form of concessional loans or aid, almost all of which
go to the public sector.[8]

Private capital does not flow to the world's poorest countries because, with rare exceptions—such as major multinationals that extract
valuable substances from the earth or from under the sea and
effectively operate like governments—investors do not receive the

legal protection they require to commit large sums of money to risky, long-term projects. Recent research in the economics of law and finance provides a composite index of the extent to which countries provide an environment that protects the rights of investors.[9] A quick comparison of how various countries fare on this index illustrates why private capital does not flow to the HIPCs and why debt forgiveness has not changed this fact. The median Brady country ranks lower than the median G-8 country on the index, but the HIPCs are not even included, because their capital markets and investor protection laws are not developed enough to even permit construction of a ranking for them. Without laws to protect their assets, potential HIPC investors remain overly exposed to risk and therefore will not invest their capital.

Poorly developed capital markets tend to go hand in hand with weak economic infrastructure more generally. Another comparison demonstrates this point. Economists Bob Hall and Chad Jones created an index useful for comparing the HIPC and Brady countries.[10] The index ranks 130 countries according to how well each country's economic infrastructure provides "an environment that supports productive activities and encourages capital accumulation, skill acquisition, invention and technology transfer."[11] A ranking of 1 indicates the most development-friendly infrastructure, and a ranking of 130 the most inimical. The median G-8 country ranks 14th, while the median Brady country is 63rd; the median HIPC comes in a distant 102nd.

The paucity of private capital flows to the world's poorest countries tells us that the concept of debt overhang is actually incongruous with the very nature of lending to them in the first place. Debt overhang and the potential for efficient debt relief that stems from its presence are predicated on the incentives and rationale that drive lending by entities seeking to maximize profits. In contrast, lending by multilateral development agencies, the overwhelming source of HIPC debt, responds to a very different set of considerations. The international commercial banks that extended loans to the Brady countries in the 1970s were private-sector institutions that expected to earn profits for their shareholders by doing so. The HIPCs' principal creditors—multilateral agencies such as the International Development Assistance arm of the World Bank—are public institutions with a broader mandate. At least part of their mission is to channel concessional loans to development projects that may yield large societal gains in the long run, but that are not immediately profitable. Since debt relief is designed to enhance efficiency in the strictly for-profit market of private-sector lending, it is not clear what benefits it brings to a largely not-for-profit set of development lending arrangements with an entirely different incentive structure.

Whereas the Brady countries suffered from debt overhang, the world's poorest countries suffer from a much more fundamental problem: they lack much of the basic infrastructure that supports profitable economic activity. It strains the imagination to believe that without the crucial foundations for profitable economic activity—everything from well-defined property rights and the rule of law to roads, schools, hospitals, and clean water—debt forgiveness will stimulate a sudden rush to the HIPCs of private foreign capital that leads to higher investment and growth, as it did in the Brady countries.

MINIMAL MAGNANIMITY

Even if it stimulates no investment or growth, does debt relief not play an important role by increasing the amount of resources available to poor countries to provide humanitarian services and build the infrastructure they need to become profitable places to invest? Is it not the case that reducing the amount of debt in poor countries would cause their net financial inflows to rise? The answer, actually, is no. When debt servicing is reduced by debt relief, the net flow of capital to poor countries does not rise; instead, grants or new loans fall. Starting with the onset of the HIPC Initiative in 1996, aid transfers from rich nations as a fraction of poor-country GDP decreased. Prior to 1996, aid to the HIPCs amounted to roughly 13.7 percent of their GDP. After 1996 that figure dropped to between 9.9 and 11.1 percent of GDP.[12]

In other words, developed countries give debt relief instead of, not in addition to, foreign aid. Debt relief is not free, and the rich countries of the world have consistently robbed Peter to pay Paul, as it were. When one of the multilateral financial institutions writes off debt, its capital base shrinks, as would happen with any other bank. Without new capital, it has less money to distribute in the form of aid or concessional loans.

The stingy arithmetic reality of debt relief applies with special force to the heralded Gleneagles Declaration of 2005. For all of the fanfare and ostensible magnanimity of the G-8 leaders toward the impoverished HIPCs, the quantity of money at stake for the developed nations of the world in the Multilateral Debt Relief Initiative was trivial. The MDRI forgave approximately US$2 billion of annual debt service payments that the HIPCs would otherwise have paid out to their multilateral creditors. Two billion dollars per year equals less than one-one-hundredth ($\frac{1}{100}$) of the quantity of official development assistance (foreign aid) pledged to poor countries by world leaders on at least three separate occasions (1970, 1992, and 2002). For the United States alone, honoring the aid pledge would provide the HIPCs with $100 billion per year. If the goal of MDRI was to increase the net flow of capital to poor countries, then it would have been far more effective for the G-8 to not forgive a single penny of debt and simply honor their aid promises.

In sum, the Gleneagles/MDRI debt cancellation announcement amounted to a feel-good moment for well-meaning advocates of debt relief and a low-cost public relations win for G-8 politicians who did nothing to increase the overall flow of resources to the world's Highly Indebted Poor Countries as a whole.

AID FOR WHOM?

It is one thing to document the stinginess of the G-8 toward poor countries. It is quite another to ask whether greater generosity would actually do any good. The history of aid flows to the developing world does not inspire confidence in the general utility of such transfer schemes. Although the amounts have not been as large as promised, rich countries have nevertheless sent billions of dollars of foreign assistance to the poorest countries on earth, and much has been made of the fact that these billions have done little, if anything, to help promote economic growth and development.[13] The late US senator Jesse Helms once likened foreign aid to pouring money down a rat hole—his uniquely blunt way of saying that aid vanishes without doing a trace of good.

In one respect, the lack of impact of aid on development and growth should come as no surprise, because foreign assistance often is not given with the intent of helping countries improve their economic performance. The United States provides a significant amount of foreign assistance for purely political reasons. Think, for instance, of the transfers from the United States to Mobutu Sese Seko, strongman of Zaire, during the Cold War. Transparency International, a global coalition against corruption, estimates that Mobutu pocketed more than US$5 billion during his reign. Is anyone really surprised that years of foreign assistance to Zaire and parallel arrangements with other countries (Egypt, for example) did not produce strong local economies?

Food aid delivered by the US Department of Agriculture (USDA) and the US Agency for International Development (USAID) through the Agricultural Trade Development Assistance Act (also known as PL 480) provides another example of extensive foreign assistance that was never intended to promote economic growth or development abroad. From its 1954 beginnings, PL 480 was widely seen as a subsidy for the US agricultural sector, a way to get rid of surpluses and open up new export markets for the benefit of US agribusinesses. And benefit they have—the US government pays up to 70 percent more than the prevailing domestic market price for corn.[14] Because food aid competes directly with farmers in the recipient countries, PL 480 depresses local prices and discourages production. Additionally, the overwhelming bias of the United States toward "tied aid"—the requirement that the aid come from US farmers, be handled by US companies, and be shipped by US carriers—makes the dominant beneficiaries of PL 480 the US agribusinesses and shipping companies that participate, not the vulnerable populations in developing countries.

In 2008 President George W. Bush asked that up to 25 percent of the food aid budget under the $290 billion farm bill be allocated to the purchase of food commodities in local and regional markets—a sensible request that could have simultaneously supported humanitarian efforts and incentivized food production in poor countries. Congress all but ignored President Bush's request, opting instead to include a $60 million, four-year pilot program to investigate the impact of the United States buying food in poor countries. For perspective, $60 million over a four-year period accounted for less than 1 percent of the estimated food aid budget from 2008 to 2012.[15]

Foreign assistance has not yet played a significant role in bringing growth to poor countries, and it has a long way to go before it could be described as anything close to efficient. But all is not lost. New research suggests that even where it does not promote economic growth, aid can help improve the quality of some lives.[16] Past failures and current research contain important clues for the design of more effective and realistic aid endeavors in the future. For instance, a large body of research that evaluates the effectiveness of antipoverty programs by using randomized trials (a technique similar to the way medical researchers test the effectiveness of new drugs) points to a potentially promising path for the use of foreign assistance.

Surveying the results of this research in their book *Poor Economics*, Abhijit Banerjee and Esther Duflo identify several areas where foreign assistance can be put to use efficiently: education (especially of girls and young women), provision of vitamin supplements, HIV prevention, spraying for malaria, and vaccination.[17] To be sure, targeting aid spending on relatively small interventions such as these is not going to transform poor countries into economic powerhouses. Applying lessons learned from the success of small-scale interventions, however, may prove valuable in developing approaches that can have economy-wide effects by helping countries deploy resources more effectively as they seek to build better schools, roads, property rights, and protections for investors. These are not easy tasks, but working toward an understanding of how to allocate aid more effectively would have a much higher cost-benefit ratio than past debt-relief efforts.

Back on Track

Sometimes economic analysis compels the head to embrace conclusions that the heart would rather not follow. With all due respect to the charities, celebrity spokespeople, and politicians who care deeply about the plight of the poor, the worldwide debt-relief campaign was a detour from the real issues at stake. Forgiving debt does not address the fundamental problem of inadequate economic systems that impede investment and growth in the world's poorest countries. And to the extent that additional resources are part of the solution, debt relief does little, if any, good. Debt relief has had a minimal (and sometimes negative) impact on net resource flows in the past, and there is little to suggest this has changed.

The story here is a hopeful one nonetheless. For a long time, HIPC economies offered their citizens little promise of a better life. Between 1970 and 1999, the average African country experienced a decline in its per capita income. That amounts to almost thirty years of falling living standards in a part of the world where grinding poverty was already a daily reality. But something changed at the turn of the century: African countries started to grow. For the first decade of the second millennium, GDP per capita in Africa increased by an average of approximately 2 percent per year. The key to maintaining this positive trend is an understanding of the forces behind it.

One contributing factor to Africa's growth renaissance is simply the fortuitous rise of export prices, which lies beyond the control of any single nation on the world's poorest continent. Many African countries produce significant quantities of copper, gold, oil, and other commodities whose prices have increased substantially as a result of surging demand for raw materials by large, rapidly growing economies like China's.

Although there is no denying that luck helps—it is good to own much of the world's copper supply while urban development in the emerging world creates a near-insatiable demand for wiring and plumbing—some countries, such as Ghana, deserve credit for the steps they have taken to stabilize their macroeconomic environments, open their economies to the benefits of free trade, and privatize inefficiently run state-owned enterprises. Economic reforms are as relevant to the HIPCs as they are to other emerging economies, and they contributed to Africa's improved economic performance. In the words of economists Laura Beny and Lisa Cook, Africa's newfound growth is the result of both metals and management.[18] Better management is, in fact, the key to creating the kinds of economic environments that can both use aid effectively and attract the private capital that Africa needs in order to sustain and accelerate its current growth trajectory. And what's good for Africa is deeply relevant for advanced nations too. Solutions to the First World problems of today can be found in Third World lessons from the past.

CHAPTER 10

TURNAROUND

TRUTH IS SOMETIMES STRANGER THAN THEATER. THE
world economy now resembles a comedic scene from an Elizabethan
play in which all of the characters have donned disguises. In the advanced nations of the world, things seem to be falling apart: the
United States is a downgraded borrower, unable to balance its budget,
while citizens of Athens and Rome have taken to the streets in protest
over the spending cuts and tax increases their governments propose to
keep national debts from spiraling out of control. Meanwhile, IMF
officials appear before emerging-market government leaders, hat in
hand, in an effort to boost their dwindling reserves. No matter how
farcical these roles may seem, the audience must suspend disbelief in
order to understand the meaning of the events onstage.

During IMF Managing Director Christine Lagarde's December
2011 visit to Brazil, the country's finance minister, Guido Mantega,
pointedly noted his country's satisfaction that "this time around the
IMF comes to Brazil not to give us money like in the past but asking
us to lend money to developed nations."[1] There is also evidence that
China and other large developing countries might be willing to offer
the IMF cash in return for the institution's agreement to adopt certain
conditions, such as giving emerging economies a bigger voting share
on the Fund's board. Apparently, IMF conditionality may soon take

on a dual meaning. Whether or not the BRIC countries end up lending money to the Fund, the die is cast. Ten years ago, nobody could have imagined serious adults in charge of the world economy even considering the possibility of the IMF and Europe receiving loans with BRIC strings attached.

Comedies of this nature usually resolve themselves with a lifting of disguises, characters switching back to their true personas, and a happy ending for all good men and women. In real life, however, emerging economies have little desire to adopt the wayward habits of the developed countries that formerly lectured them. Nor is it clear that the proud First World countries that once stood at the front of the Third World classroom are ready to take a seat and listen. But listen they must, because if advanced economies are to engineer a turnaround, restoring jobs, hope, and cash to their increasingly despondent middle and working classes, they will have to do so through shared sacrifice and disciplined policies that put commitment to the future ahead of political expediency and short-lived gain.

THE FOUNDATION FOR GROWTH

While growth miracles of the kind that occurred in East Asia during the 1960s, 1970s, and 1980s are few and far between, it is all too easy for policy mistakes to cause massive, extended economic contractions that can devastate a country's standard of living in less than a generation. In developing countries, any decline in the standard of living can be a matter of life and death, spelling the difference between whether children get enough to eat and have a chance to go to school or end up begging on the streets. The consequences of policy mistakes in advanced nations are typically not so dire, but falling incomes in developed-world countries do exact a substantial human toll: unemployment, erosion of work skills, home foreclosures, and the loss of dignity that sets in when people are unable to provide for their families.

Instead of trying to orchestrate miracles, leaders should focus on avoiding mistakes. Because economic activity does not implode in countries with low inflation and modest debt, providing a stable macroeconomic environment is the first rule of good policy.

The need for stability was a central theme in the "Program for Sustained Growth" that James Baker unveiled nearly thirty years ago. The economic reform agenda eventually known as the Washington Consensus encouraged Third World countries to stabilize their economies in order to improve efficiency and lay the foundation for additional reforms that would also contribute to faster growth. Reasonable people can disagree about the appropriateness of the manner in which the agenda was applied, but the history of the developing world tells us that where economic reforms were adopted and sustained, they increased efficiency and created value.

The analysis at the heart of this book, conducted through the forward-looking lens of the stock market as well as the backward-looking frame of traditional economic indicators like growth and inflation, provides several important lessons for both developed and developing countries in search of stability and growth.

First, anyone who speaks of the Washington Consensus as though it were a single package of reforms to be applied uniformly regardless of circumstances is either misinformed or acting in bad faith. In fact, no country has followed the Consensus in its entirety, and no serious economist would argue that any country should. In debating the best method of promoting prosperity, we should ask not whether the Washington Consensus worked or failed, but which elements from the menu of potential policies have worked in which contexts, which showed promise but were implemented too swiftly or rigidly, and which provide the greatest impact per unit of political capital expended.

It is also true that we must be wary of those who seize on a particular malady and insist that it become the central focus of economic policy. There is no more urgent example of this than the fiscal hawks circling in the wake of the recent recession. Whereas austerity measures succeeded in creating stable economic environments in many developing countries that suffered from high inflation, disappointing outcomes in the context of moderate inflation suggest that a gradual approach to deficit reduction may be best where inflation is not the primary concern. When it comes to liberalization, we know from the principle of comparative advantage that all nations can benefit from free trade, but leaders must remember that their countries need both imports and exports in order to thrive. Protectionism only gets in the way. The case for trade in goods extends to trade in capital, but countries should proceed with caution here, remembering the critical distinction between debt and equity. Opening a country's stock market to foreign shareholders reduces the cost of capital, drives up wages, and can be an important vehicle for facilitating privatization and foreign direct investment; in contrast, rapid liberalization of debt financing from abroad almost always ends in crises.

Data and analysis can tell us what kinds of policies are most likely to help countries grow. But without a sustained, disciplined application of those policies—that is, without a pragmatic growth strategy that favors the long term and is executed with temperance, vigilance, and flexibility—nations will underachieve. To avoid economic underperformance, leaders must reject the dysfunctional politics we currently see in many world capitals. Discipline has two facets: in economic policy as in life, how you conduct yourself during the journey is at least as important as the path you choose to take. During the last century, the First World taught developing countries *what* they needed to do in order to prosper. In this new millennium, the Third World has many lessons to impart to advanced nations about *how* to implement the right policies—with wisdom, character, and a strong commitment to the future, even in the face of present-day political constraints.

THIRD WORLD ANTS,
FIRST WORLD GRASSHOPPERS

When Andres Velasco became Chile's minister of finance in March 2006, the country's treasury held $6 billion in savings. Over the next two years, that number ballooned to almost $50 billion as the worldwide commodity boom drove up the price of copper, Chile's major export. The country's good fortune did not go unnoticed—nor did the absence of a commensurate increase in public spending. In November 2008, thousands of protesters burned an effigy of Velasco in the streets of Santiago, vilifying him for refusing to share the treasury's riches. Velasco held his ground, resisting the push for greater spending and higher public-sector wages while reminding those calling for his resignation that the copper-generated surplus was money for a rainy day.

As the world economy plunged deep into recession in 2009, the wisdom of Velasco's tough choices became abundantly clear. The crisis curtailed access to credit and forced many countries to endure belt-tightening, but Chile used its arsenal of savings to launch a $4 billion package of tax cuts to cushion the impact of the global slowdown on its economy and to distribute a raft of subsidies to mitigate the hardships of the poor. By April 2009, Velasco was the most popular minister in President Michelle Bachelet's cabinet, with an approval rating of 57 percent—almost double what it had been in August of the previous year.[2]

If Chile and other developing countries are the prudent ant in Aesop's classic fable, then advanced economies are in many ways the profligate grasshopper. In September 1999, the United States achieved a record budget surplus; it would do even better a year later with a net intake of $236 billion.[3] In those flush times, the two men who vied to succeed President Clinton engaged in a vigorous debate over whether to return the surplus to the American people or put the money in a social security lockbox.

George W. Bush won the election, declared before a joint session of Congress that "the surplus is the people's money," and pursued a series of tax cuts over the course of his first term in office that put the country on a path to deficits. The recession that hit the U.S. economy in 2001 probably would have triggered deficits no matter what course of policy the country pursued. But without tax cuts, the deficits would probably have been smaller, and the United States would have had a larger financial cushion to help it cope with the heightened military spending that followed the terrorist attack of September 11, 2001.[4] It is also worth asking whether the United States might have avoided coming dangerously close to defaulting on its debt, roiling financial markets, and losing its AAA credit rating in the summer of 2011 if President Bush had pursued a more temperate fiscal policy. This is not a partisan point. With hindsight, we know that either a Bush or a Gore administration would have faced the need for increased spending on national security. Would Gore's policies have put the country in a better position to deal with the unanticipated shock of 9/11? It is not unreasonable to think that the answer is no. Although the surplus that could have provided a welcome fiscal cushion was eliminated by Bush's tax cuts, under Gore it might have been eroded by an increase in domestic spending.

Every leader would like to have money to address urgent needs during hard times. The real question is whether they have the discipline required to save their fiscal surpluses when the economy is doing well—as per Chile—so that they can run deficits when times are lean without having to worry about the national debt getting so large that financial markets tank. Beyond the United States, advanced nations like Portugal, Italy, Greece, and Spain almost certainly would have been better off if they had been more frugal in good times. For ideas about how to revive European economies, it is time to consider Caribbean lessons for Club Med.

"Long Road Draw Sweat, Shortcut Draw Blood"

The people of the Caribbean share a well-known maxim, so poignant and descriptive as expressed in broken English that it transcends culture and almost needs no explanation: "Long road draw sweat, shortcut draw blood." Taking the long road—doing something the right way—requires hard work but generally produces results of lasting value. Shortcuts feel good in the present moment but invariably unravel, causing much pain and suffering. I heard this saying many times as a child, and more pointedly from my father during my teenage years. The leaders of France, Germany, and other European nations would have done well to internalize its meaning at the birth of the euro.

The European Monetary Union consists of seventeen countries bound by a common market, common money, and a common problem: monetary union without fiscal union—that is, without credible commitments from countries to keep their deficits under control. By introducing the euro in 1999, the European Monetary Union hoped to deliver efficiency gains to member countries by creating a single currency to accompany the single market, thus eliminating the need to change currencies to buy and sell goods within Europe and avoiding exchange-rate fluctuations, and strengthening price stability. The problem has been that in the rush to make the vision for the euro a reality, European leaders adopted a single currency before all the members of the Union were in compliance with the conditions for entry they had established some seven years earlier.

The Maastricht Treaty of 1992 laid out four ostensibly strict criteria that countries needed to meet in the areas of inflation, fiscal policy, exchange rates, and interest rates in order to accede to the euro and make sure that their economies were strong enough to keep up with the other members of the club. Fiscal standards proved trickiest.

History and theory suggested that a ceiling of 3 percent on the government deficit as a fraction of GDP would prevent the stock of government IOUs from growing faster than the underlying economies that had to service the debt. Total government debt as a fraction of GDP was not to exceed 60 percent. When it came time to apply the entrance criteria, however, Maastricht's bark was worse than its bite. Seven of the twelve original members of the zone were granted entry at the outset of the euro despite having debt-to-GDP ratios in excess of 60 percent.[5]

Once admitted to the euro, countries were supposed to abide by the Stability and Growth Pact (SGP), a framework established in 1997 to keep countries from breaching the already compromised fiscal standards they should have met for entry. The European Commission was given the task of monitoring the debts and deficits of euro members and issuing warnings and eventually sanctions to countries in violation of the deficit and debt ceilings. Ironically, the two countries that pushed most fervently for the SGP, Germany and France, found themselves in violation of the pact in 2003.

The European Commission recommended that France and Germany reduce their deficits to comply with the SGP. Facing the threat of an embarrassing public slap on the wrist from the European Commission, Germany and France used their outsized influence on the Economic and Financial Affairs Council of the European Union to stop the European Commission's recommendation from becoming official.[6] By blocking the Commission's ability to "name and shame" countries in violation of the deficit rules, France and Germany eviscerated the SGP, setting the stage for countries like Portugal, Italy, Greece, and Spain to pursue the path of profligacy with a sense of impunity.

The European shortcut of forming a monetary union before all members had reached compliance with the standards for entry contrasts sharply with the tale of tiny Barbados in the 1990s. Faced with a scenario that resembled the current European situation—anger over the prospect of wage cuts and fiscal austerity—but clearly needing to act or have actions thrust upon them, the leaders of Barbados took steps that were bold, sensible, and consistent with the policy of maintaining the country's fixed exchange rate. Once they determined the right course of policy, they followed the long road of forging a social compact between employers, trade unions, and the government. In particular, rather than locking themselves into a lifestyle they could not afford, they reached an agreement to base future wage increases on productivity gains. When productivity rises in concert with wages, everybody wins: the workers' standard of living rises, and firms maintain profitability. Rather than fighting over a shrinking pie, negotiations focus on the equitable way to divide a growing pie.

Of course, there are important differences between Europe and the Caribbean. The population of Barbados and all the islands of the Eastern Caribbean combined is still smaller than the country of Estonia. The quantities of capital flows in and out of the region are also negligible in comparison to capital flows in Europe. These limitations notwithstanding, the fact remains that both Barbados and the Eastern Caribbean Currency Area have maintained fixed exchange rates for almost forty years. I am not advocating for fixed rates, but if a country decides that a fixed exchange rate is part of its economic strategy—as is clearly the case with countries in the euro zone vis-à-vis each other—then it must have the discipline to abide by policies that are internally consistent with the vision.

The story of growth in the developing world is one of sustained commitment to creating a better life for current and future generations. In Barbados, implementing tough measures to cut workers' wages was necessary to regain export competitiveness and revive the island's economy. In China, steady, pragmatic experimentation with reforms transformed an inefficient collectivist economy into a modern-day juggernaut. And in Brazil, policies to end monetization of the deficit and reduce government spending put an end to astronomical inflation and paved the way for growth.

Relationships Matter

Having taken the long road to economic success, a number of former Third World countries now find themselves in the hall of prospering nations, only to be pushed aside by those who refuse to fully recognize and reward their hard-won gains. Not enough room has been made for developing nations at the tables of global summits where key decisions about international economic policy are made. Adding insult to injury, the rich but slow-growing advanced countries also appear unwilling or unable to wean themselves from a variety of policy shortcuts that contributed to a hemorrhaging of global financial markets in 2008, that undermine the credibility of the euro, and that threaten to jeopardize the future of the entire world economy. Cooperation and consensus are crucial to shared prosperity. Without these, many potential gains will go unrealized—the collapse of the World Trade Organization's Doha Development Round being but one recent example of opportunities lost.

In 2009 the First World took a step toward greater inclusion of emerging markets by expanding the forum for discussions of international economic coordination from the G-8, which had been responsible for convening discussions on major policy issues, to include the G-20. Membership in this premier forum enables countries to influence the direction of the global economic agenda. The move to invite a number of developing countries like Brazil, China, and India into this highly visible leadership position was a gracious gesture, but its real impact has been minimal. We have yet to see the First World embrace any change at the IMF, the World Bank, or the WTO that substantively acknowledges the increased importance of emerging nations to the world economy.

For instance, leaders at the G-20 summit in London in April 2009 issued a communiqué committing to reforms in the governance of the international financial institutions that would "reflect changes in the world economy and the new challenges of globalization. . . .

Emerging and developing countries, including the poorest, must have greater voice and representation." But in spite of this declaration, the share of votes on the IMF Executive Board remains disproportionately skewed in favor of Europe and against the emerging world. Brazil, Russia, India, China, and South Africa account for roughly 20 percent of the world's economic output but have only 11 percent of the votes on the IMF board. The countries of the European Union account for 24 percent of world output but hold 32 percent of board votes.[7] Furthermore, with almost 18 percent of all votes, the United States has veto power over board decisions that require 85 percent approval.

Given the glacial pace of First World movement on issues of international economic coordination and governance, emerging economies have begun applying pressure through their newfound power of the purse. As Brazil's finance minister, Guido Mantega, emphasized in his remarks to Christine Lagarde, "The BRICs are ready to strengthen the IMF, but this depends on [the IMF] doing the tasks they set out to do."[8] This is where a little goodwill goes a long way. Advanced nations need to recognize that fair play and proper inclusion of emerging nations in the global economic dialogue not only is good form but will bolster developing countries' resolve to continue embracing market-friendly policies. Their ability and willingness to do so can only contribute to worldwide stability, jobs, and growth for all.

STAYING THE COURSE

Developing countries have come a long way since the heyday of dependency theory, when runaway inflation, import substitution, hostility to foreign capital, and a productive sector dominated by state-owned enterprises were the order of the day. Of their own volition in a few cases, but largely as a result of external forces and actors (ranging from devastating debt crises to the US Treasury and the IMF), the nations formerly known as the Third World adopted a different approach to economic policy that eventually earned them a new name and new prospects. Yet even as these "emerging economies" move to the head of the class, setting the standard for good policy on several counts, they would do well to keep in mind a number of lessons they themselves have learned along the way.

First and foremost, developing countries must be careful not to reject ideas about how to make their economies more efficient simply because the ideas come from a source they find hard to take. Having battled their way through the Third World Debt Crisis in the 1980s and the subsequent financial crises in emerging markets in the 1990s, many developing countries are sick and tired of the IMF and the World Bank doling out policy advice that its American and European shareholders are not willing to follow. As infuriating as it is to have someone command, "Do as I say, not as I do," countries should not hesitate to comply with those pieces of advice that are in their national interest. As Nobel Laureate V. S. Naipaul emphasized in his 1990 Walter B. Wriston Lecture, "Our Universal Civilization," certain principles transcend ownership by any culture.[9] Naipaul's argument applies to modern economics just as powerfully as it does to his discussion of the pursuit of happiness. Adopting policy reforms that improve the functioning of your economy does not make you a Washington "sellout" any more than breathing makes you an Anglophile because oxygen was discovered by English clergyman Joseph Priestley. Sometimes the best policy choice really is the one recommended to you.

Of course, the trick lies in distinguishing correctly between reforms that are in the national interest and those that are not. If the recommendations being made seem unpalatable or go against the landscape of the local economy, the lesson is simple: be prepared when you come to the table for discussions. When you need help from multilateral institutions to pay your bills, you cannot expect to get money if you simply oppose their plans for economic restructuring. Like the Barbadians who resisted devaluation and implemented an across-the-board wage cut instead, or South Korea whose export-led growth strategy involved a gradual and selective reduction in trade barriers rather than a carte blanche opening up, countries must propose constructive and viable alternatives if they want to be taken seriously.

After proposing their own economic restructuring and growth strategies, countries need to implement policies that are consistent with their plans—and they need to stick with them over time. This point may be nothing more than a corollary to the "long road" adage, but it bears emphasis nonetheless. Not even the most successful emerging economies, however much they have to teach the First World, can afford to throw caution to the wind and abandon years of accretive steps toward excellence.

ALL TOGETHER NOW

There are many important aspects of development and the global economy that I have not discussed in this book—the importance of empowering women, the promise of micro finance, the challenge of HIV, and the threat of climate change, to name a few. These are important topics, but without growth it will be harder to deal with any of them. Growth is not a sufficient condition for development, but it is absolutely necessary. Without growth, life becomes a series of zero-sum struggles by individuals and countries trying to preserve their share of limited resources. With growth, the pie expands and the politics of spending priorities no longer involve such stark trade-offs.

In his classic book *The Theory of Economic Growth*, the late Nobel Laureate Sir Arthur Lewis reminded us that growth does not necessarily make people happier, but by releasing them from the drudgery of life's menial tasks, it does confer a certain freedom that comes from having a wider range of choices. This was the case for growth when Lewis published his masterpiece in 1955, and it remains so today.

Judiciously applied, reforms increase the sustainable level of goods and services that a country can produce with its resources. There is no

TURNAROUND
doubt, however, that the process can be wrenching, because increasing productive efficiency generates losers as well as winners. In principle, the overall income gains to society will be large enough to make it possible to negotiate sufficient compensation for losers to overcome their objections to reforms. Yet some societies may choose to forgo reform in order to sidestep the political bargaining between winners and losers altogether. They may choose to live with economic arrangements that sacrifice some productive efficiency in order to achieve less income inequality. This is their choice, of course, but countries that opt to live with more inefficiency need to accept slower (or no) increases in their standard of living or markets will eventually force them to live within their means.

Much of the Third World has evolved. We can only hope that in the global economic drama unfolding before our eyes, the First World, having donned the robes of Third World economies past, will soon acknowledge that much of the Third World has in fact moved on. If the Third World continues to set the example of making disciplined choices, the First World follows its lead, and we all find a way to work together in the name of mutual self-interest, then the entire world may yet see a promising denouement.

ACKNOWLEDGMENTS

In the process of bringing *Turnaround* to life, I have benefited from the help of two extraordinary editors. Tim Bartlett, senior executive editor at Basic Books, had the vision to move me beyond a synthesis of theories, facts, and figures about emerging economies to the larger story of transformation and interconnectedness that lies behind the logic of economic models. Allison Cay Parker, my developmental editor, is a coach without equal. Demanding, kind, and skilled, she made sure I did what I said I was going to do and refused to sign off until I did it properly. Without Allison, this book would not exist.

I would also like to thank my agent, Andrew Wylie. From our very first meeting, he saw this book for what it could be and never looked back. I am also grateful to Rimjhim Dey for providing support in matters of book publicity.

Turnaround experienced its very own transformation due to the extraordinary generosity of numerous colleagues and friends. Jessica Einhorn, Stan Fischer, Anne Krueger, and Bob Solow read through the entire manuscript at an early stage and shared extensive comments that sharpened my reasoning. Paul Romer provided vital input to key chapters, all the while insisting that it is possible to communicate complicated economic arguments in plain English. Will Baumol pushed me to think harder about Barbados and Jamaica; DeLisle Worrell provided firsthand insight into the events surrounding the wage-price protocol in Barbados. My conversations with Bob Kavesh and Andrei Shleifer ensured that this remained a book about people as well as ideas. Thanks also to Marie Dixon, Colin Flavin, Grace Garnice, Kristen Harrison, Julia Nasev, Charlotte Pace, Davida Pines, Nancy Rappaport, Martha Simmons, and Gail Steinberg—all particularly fine people whose ideas made a real difference in the final manuscript. The Reverend Kitty Lehman and participants in the Breaking Bread at Bede's dinner and lecture series were early supporters, along with the late Diana Kirk.

E. B. White said that writing is difficult and bad for the disposition. During the past three years, I have learned that his observation applies most forcefully to the writing one does in the wee hours before coming to work. I am accordingly grateful to my colleagues in the Dean's Office at NYU Stern, particularly Anastasia Crosswhite, Anna Davitt, and Beth Murray, for their consistent forbearance and good humor with this inveterate scribbler. I would also like to thank John Sexton, Marty Lipton, and Dave McLaughlin for encouraging me to think of scholarship and leadership as complements, not substitutes. I am a better dean for writing this book and a more effective writer for being dean.

The writing in this book has its genesis in the work I've done with several people. My longtime friend and coauthor Anusha Chari draws special thanks for her patience with me, as my devotion to *Turnaround* slowed our progress on several projects. The fingerprints of my writings and conversations with Anusha are all over this book. My work with Serkan Arslanalp, Matthew Clair, Sandile Hlatshwayo, Prakash Kannan, Peter Lorentzen, Conrad Miller, and Diego Sasson also plays a central role in the story. Additionally, I owe a debt of gratitude to Matt and Sandile, along with Calah Singleton, for their superb assistance in performing a range of tasks related to background research for the book. Sandy Berg provided tireless assistance typing up scores of handwritten notes.

The research on which this book is based could not have happened without the generous financial support of many. I wish to thank the

National Science Foundation, the Ford Foundation, the National Bureau of Economic Research, and the Brookings Institution. At NYU: Bill Berkley, in whose eponymous faculty chair I sit, and the Richard R. West Chair. And at Stanford: John A. and Cynthia Fry Gunn for their generous faculty fellowship, the Stanford Institute for Economic Policy Research, the Stanford Center for International Development, the Center for Democracy Development and the Rule of Law in the Freeman Spogli Institute, the Hoover Institution, and the Center for Global Business and the Economy.

Turnaround is the culmination of two decades' worth of research. For nurturing my intellectual and career development, I would like to thank Olivier Blanchard, Jeremy Bulow, Steve Buser, Sandy Darity, the late Rudi Dornbusch, Dick Eckaus, Gene Flood, Reed Hundt, Bob Joss, Don Lessard, Jim Poterba, Mike Spence, Jeremy Stein, René Stulz, Ewart Thomas, and Jim Van Horne. I would also like to thank David Kreps for encouraging me to pursue my goal of writing a book, and Sir K. Dwight Venner for giving me the summer job that led to my writing this one in particular.

Of all the blessings that come with university life, teaching is first among equals. A number of undergraduates and graduate students at NYU, Stanford, and MIT have contributed greatly to my understanding of the world by collecting data, challenging my ideas, and asking me questions to which I did not know the answer. I am grateful to Rania Eltom, Christina Flood, Begna Gebreyes, Mina Hardy, Nan Li, Chad Milner, Cecilia Mo, Karen Saah, Laura Veldkamp, Richard Walsh, and Aminah West for their assistance.

I could never have completed Turnaround without the love, support, and patience of my wife, Lisa, and our four boys, Christian, Langston, Hayden, and Harrison. They all deserve a king's ransom for suffering a husband and father who devoted three years' worth of their weekends to the solitary task of writing. Raising four sons while writing a book requires a team effort. Lisa's parents, Elbert and

Blondean Nelson, were always there to help at key moments. Lisa and I are also grateful to Morena Monge, Irma Salinas, and Ana Pereira, who have watched over and cared for our children as though they were their own.

Finally, my deepest gratitude goes to my mom, whose unflagging support compelled her to wade through early drafts of the manuscript, even as she was mourning the passing of my father. Dad, this book is for you.

NOTES

Introduction

1. In at least one country, the United States, the recession actually began in December 2007, but in the interest of avoiding confusion I will follow the convention of referring to the "recession of 2008–2009."

2. Surowiecki, *The Wisdom of Crowds.*

3. Shiller, *Irrational Exuberance,* p. 189.

4. This statement follows immediately from a vast literature in financial economics that demonstrates that stock prices respond to news. See MacKinlay, "Event Studies in Economics and Finance."

5. Kaminsky and Reinhart, "The Twin Crises."

6. Latinobarómetro conducted the survey. See Lora, Panizza, and Quispe-Agnoli, "Reform Fatigue."

Chapter 1

1. Sachs, "Managing the LDC Debt Crisis."

2. Reagan, "Remarks to Employees of the Department of the Treasury."

3. Baker, statement before the annual meetings of the International Monetary Fund and the World Bank Group.

4. Rodrik, "Goodbye Washington Consensus, Hello Washington Confusion?"

5. Naím, "Washington Consensus or Washington Confusion?" p. 90.

6. Williamson, speech delivered at the Center for Strategic and International Studies.

7. Chavez, speech delivered to the United Nations.

8. Stiglitz, *Globalization and Its Discontents*.

9. Stiglitz, "A Global Agenda for Employment."

10. Rodrik, "Goodbye Washington Consensus, Hello Washington Confusion?," p. 975.

11. Krueger, "Meant Well, Tried Little, Failed Much."

12. Gil Díaz, "Don't Blame Our Failures on Reforms That Have Not Taken Place."

13. Noonan, "This Is No Time for Moderation."

Chapter 2

1. Levi, *Michael Manley*, p. 157.

2. See also Acemoglu, Johnson, and Robinson, "The Colonial Origins of Comparative Development: An Empirical Investigation."

3. La Porta, Lopez-de-Silanes, and Shleifer, "The Economic Consequences of Legal Origins."

4. Henry and Miller, "Institutions vs. Policies: A Tale of Two Islands."

5. The inflation-adjusted index, or "real" GDP per capita, is 100 in 1960, so that its natural log is 4.6. By 2011 the natural log is 5.6 for Barbados and 5.1 for Jamaica, so the average growth rate of real GDP per capita for Barbados is 2.0 percent per year versus 1.0 percent per year for Jamaica.

6. Bertram, "Revisiting Michael Manley's Social Revolution."

7. Stone and Wellisz, "Jamaica," p. 176.

8. Bertram, "Revisiting Michael Manley's Social Revolution."

9. Stone and Wellisz, "Jamaica," p. 180.

10. Bertram, "Revisiting Michael Manley's Social Revolution."

11. Payne, *Politics in Jamaica*.

12. Massaquoi, "*Ebony* Interview with Jamaica Prime Minister Michael Manley."

13. Levitt, *Reclaiming Development*, p. 271.

14. Wint, *Competitiveness in Small Developing Economies: Insights from the Caribbean*, p. 48.

15. Robotham, "Learning from Barbados."

16. Kaminsky and Reinhart, "The Twin Crises"; MacKinlay, "Event Studies in Economics and Finance."

Chapter 3

1. Broad, "How About a Real Solution to Third World Debt?"

2. Volcker, remarks before the sixty-third annual meeting of the Bankers' Association for Foreign Trade.

3. The original fifteen countries were Argentina, Bolivia, Brazil, Chile, Colombia, Côte d'Ivoire, Ecuador, Mexico, Morocco, Nigeria, Peru, the Philippines, Uruguay, Venezuela, and Yugoslavia. Costa Rica and Jamaica were added later.

4. See the Public Papers of President Ronald W. Reagan, available at http://www.reagan.utexas.edu/archives/speeches/publicpapers.html.

5. Bruno and Easterly, "Inflation Crises and Long-Run Growth."

6. Reed, "Hyperinflation Threatens Brazil."

7. Tanzi, "Inflation, Lags in Collection, and the Real Value of Tax Revenue."

8. Henry and Kannan, "Growth and Returns in Emerging Markets."

9. Chari, Henry, and Sasson, "Capital Market Integration and Wages." See also Henry, "Capital Account Liberalization, the Cost of Capital, and Economic Growth," and "Capital Account Liberalization: Theory, Evidence, and Speculation."

10. Henry and Kannan, "Growth and Returns in Emerging Markets."

Chapter 4

1. IMF, *World Economic Outlook: Rebalancing Growth*, p. 2.

2. Reinhart and Rogoff, *This Time Is Different*.

3. Holderith, "The Myth of Developed Market Multinationals as Emerging Market Investment Surrogates"; see also Coca-Cola, 10K filing with the Securities and Exchange Commission, February 2009, p. 14.

4. Wentz, "Top 100 Global Advertisers Heap Their Spending Abroad"; Sewell, "Procter & Gamble Aims to Add 1 Billion Customers"; CNN Money, "Procter & Gamble: Fortune 500 Rankings 2011"; ADVFN, "Intel Company Financial Information."

5. Shleifer, "The Age of Milton Friedman."

6. Brazil and much of Latin America also experienced strong growth from 1964 to 1974, but progress slowed dramatically over the next decade as a result of extensive government intervention in the economy and unsustainable borrowing that culminated in the Third World Debt Crisis.

7. Bottelier, "China and the World Bank," p. 4.

8. Yergin and Stanislaw, *The Commanding Heights*, p. 189.

9. Ibid.

10. Pregelj, "Most-Favored-Nation Trade Status of the People's Republic of China."

11. *The Economist*, "The New Titans."

12. See Wilson and Purushothaman, "Dreaming with BRICs: The Path to 2050."

13. O'Neil, Wilson, Purushothaman, and Stupnytska, "How Solid Are the BRICs?"

14. Nessman, "Indian Strike Against Reforms Shuts Trains, Shops."

15. Flock, "Ngozi Okonjo-Iweala, World Bank Presidential Candidate, Says She Would Focus on Job Creation."

16. IMF, "Quota and Voting Shares Before and After Implementation of Reforms Agreed in 2008 and 2010."

17. Times Live, "Trevor Manuel Slams Europe's IMF Hold."

18. See, for example, Spilimbergo et al., "Fiscal Policy for the Crisis."

19. Colombia, Poland, and Mexico accessed the FCL, but none of these countries had actually used any of the money at the time this book went to press; see IMF, "Factsheet: The IMF's Flexible Credit Line (FCL)."

Chapter 5

1. Carnegy, "Germany Must Accept Growth Pact Says Hollande."

2. Cowell and Kulish, "Austerity Faces Sharper Debate."

3. Some scholars question the validity of this belief. See, for example, Sargent, "The Ends of Four Big Inflations."

4. The current shortfall between taxes and spending, including interest payments and amortization on past debt.

5. See Thomas, *From Inside Brazil*, p. 188.

6. Henry, "Is Disinflation Good for the Stock Market?"

7. On December 14, 1989, Chile returned to democracy with the election of Patricio Aylwin as president. Aylwin served from 1990 to 1994.

8. Corbo, "Monetary Policy and Central Bank Independence in Chile," p. 5.

9. For data, see Aninat, "Chile in the 1990s."

10. Blanchard and Cotarelli, "Ten Commandments for Fiscal Adjustment in Advanced Economies."

11. Palmer and Bosley, "IMF Shows New Flexibility on Fiscal Austerity."

Chapter 6

1. Readers familiar with the academic field of international trade will recognize some of the ideas in this paragraph and the next from the theory of modern comparative advantage as articulated, for example, by Helpman and Krugman in *Market Structure and Foreign Trade*. Modern comparative advantage tells us that the pattern of international trade for developing countries need not be determined

solely by their endowments of natural resources. Economies of scale and scope and learning by doing can also play an important role.

2. Biggs, "Electronics: A Mainstay of Korean Economy."

3. Kelkar, "India's Emerging Economic Challenges."

4. See Wacziarg and Welch, "Trade Liberalization and Growth: New Evidence."

5. Average tariff rates in developing countries fell from 28 percent in the period 1980–1985 to 15 percent in 2000. Exports as a percentage of GDP rose from 13 percent in 1980 to about 24 percent in 2001 (World Bank, "Something Special About the 1990s?," p. 65).

6. See Rodríguez and Rodrik, "Trade Policy and Economic Growth."

7. For an extensive discussion of the arguments in favor of the before-and-after approach to studying policy changes, see Henry, "Capital Account Liberalization."

8. See Wacziarg and Welch, "Trade Liberalization and Growth: New Evidence."

9. For trade liberalization dates, except Jordan, see ibid. Jordan's date comes from Risager, "On the Effects of Trade Policy Reform: The Case of Jordan." In "Trade Liberalization and Growth in Developing Countries," Anne Krueger reports that South Korea began easing trade restrictions in 1960 and Turkey began opening trade in 1980. I believe that these earlier dates conflict with those reported by Wacziarg and Welch because Wacziarg and Welch report the date on which countries began an *uninterrupted* move toward free trade.

10. Jordan was the only country to have negative returns.

11. See Henry, "Stock Market Liberalization, Economic Reform, and Emerging Market Equity Prices."

12. See Corbo and Fischer, "Structural Adjustment, Stabilization, and Policy Reform"; Krueger, "Trade Liberalization and Growth in Developing Countries."

13. Krueger, "Trade Liberalization and Growth in Developing Countries."

14. Kim, *Learning and Innovation in Economic Development*, p. 360; Kim, "The Dynamics of Technology Development."

15. Dornbusch, "The Case for Trade Liberalization in Developing Countries."

16. Krueger, "East Asian Growth Experience and Endogenous Growth Theory," p. 12.

17. Amsden, *Asia's Next Giant*, p. 80.

18. Global Trade Alert, *Tensions Contained . . . For Now.*

19. Fairtrade Foundation, *The Great Cotton Stitch-Up.*

Chapter 7

1. The distinction between savings and investment bears mentioning, because people often refer to household "investment" in the stock market or other financial instruments when they should speak of savings. Saving occurs when a worker deposits a check in his bank account or some other financial asset and does not spend it. Investment happens when a company allocates the savings channeled to them in the form of debt or equity to increase the productive capacity of the economy, implementing projects such as building a new factory or installing a new machine.

2. *Time*, "Mining: Nationalization in Zambia."

3. Copper production fell from a peak of 750,000 metric tons per year in 1973 to 226,192 in the year 2000. See US Department of State, "Background Note: Zambia."

4. Walters, "Failure of Zambia's Nationalisation Programme."

5. *Time*, "Business: IBM Withdraws from India."

6. Martell and Stulz, "Equity-Market Liberalizations as Country IPOs."

7. Twomey, "Patterns of Foreign Investment in the Third World in the Twentieth Century."

8. Kotkin, "First World, Third World (Maybe Not in That Order)."

9. Kanaan, "Tanzania's Experience with Trade Liberalization."

10. IMF, "United Republic of Tanzania: Financial System Stability Assessment Update."

11. Mwasalwiba, Dahles, and Wakkee, "Graduate Entrepreneurship in Tanzania."

12. *Forbes*, "One Cost of the Chilean Capital Controls."

13. See, for example, Farnsworth, "Micro-Loans to the World's Poorest."

14. Singapore Election, "How Forced CPF Savings Help PAP to Generate 'High' Growth Rates."

15. Dernberger, "Economic Realities."

16. Stein, *What I Think: Essays on Economics, Politics, and Life*, p. 32.

17. Rudolph et al., "A Global Fire Sale."

18. For a detailed discussion of the opening-up process, see Henry, "Capital Account Liberalization: Theory, Evidence, and Speculation."

19. Organization for Economic Cooperation and Development, *OECD Benchmark Definition of Foreign Direct Investment*.

20. Chari, Ouimet, and Tesar, "Acquiring Control in Emerging Markets."

21. See Henry, "Stock Market Liberalization, Economic Reform, and Emerging Market Equity Prices."

22. See Martell and Stulz, "Equity-Market Liberalizations as Country IPOS."

23. See Henry, "Capital Account Liberalization, the Cost of Capital, and Economic Growth."

24. See Chari, Henry, and Sasson, "Capital Market Integration and Wages."

25. See Henry, "Capital Account Liberalization: Theory, Evidence, and Speculation."

Chapter 8

1. WDI Indicators, 2009; see also Wheat, "The Fall of the Peso and the Mexican 'Miracle.'"

2. Short-term, dollar-denominated bank loans played a significant role in the Asian crisis.

3. See Bhagwati, "The Capital Myth"; Rodrik, "Who Needs Capital-Account Convertibility?"; Stiglitz, *Globalization and Its Discontents.*

4. Bulow, "First World Governments and Third World Debt"; Rogoff, "International Institutions for Reducing Global Financial Instability"; Obstfeld, "The Global Capital Market: Benefactor or Menace?"

5. Henry and Lorentzen, "Domestic Capital Market Reform and Access to Global Finance."

6. Henry, "Capital Account Liberalization: Theory, Evidence, and Speculation."

7. Sachs, *Theoretical Issues in International Borrowing;* Krugman, "Financing vs. Forgiving a Debt Overhang"; Sachs, "Introduction"; Eaton and Gersovitz, "Debt with Potential Repudiation."

8. Rose and Spiegel, "A Gravity Model of Sovereign Lending."

9. For a more extended discussion of the menu of options involved in the Brady Plan, see Arslanalp and Henry, "Is Debt Relief Efficient?"

10. Ibid.

11. The capital stock growth numbers are calculated using data from Bosworth and Collins, "The Empirics of Growth."

Chapter 9

1. This startling fact, as well as some of the language contained in this paragraph, may be recognizable to some readers because it first appeared in a chapter about debt relief and aid that I coauthored with Serkan Arslanalp. See Arslanalp and Henry, "Helping the Poor to Help Themselves."

2. See Speth, "Debt Relief, Yes, but Development Aid as Well." For details on the completion points, see Arslanalp and Henry, "Policy Watch: Debt Relief," and the G-24 Secretariat briefing paper on the HIPC Initiative.

3. The Vatican, "Bull of Indiction of the Great Jubilee of the Year 2000."

4. Following the meeting in Cologne, the G-8 issued a statement calling for "faster, broader, and deeper debt relief." The meeting led to the creation of the Enhanced HIPC Initiative, under which sixteen additional countries reached their completion points and began receiving debt relief in 2000. See G-8 Secretariat, "G-7 Statement."

5. Henry, testimony before the Senate Committee on Foreign Relations.

6. Based on the following calculation: net resource transfer = new lending + grants + portfolio equity + foreign direct investment – debt service – dividend payments.

7. Arslanalp and Henry, "Policy Watch: Debt Relief."

8. Ibid.

9. La Porta et al., "Legal Determinants of External Finance."

10. Hall and Jones, "Why Do Some Countries Produce So Much More Output per Worker Than Others?"

11. Ibid., p. 84.

12. Arslanalp and Henry, "Policy Watch: Debt Relief."

13. Easterly, "Can Foreign Aid Buy Growth?"

14. Murphy and McAfee, *US Food Aid: Time to Get It Right*.

15. In 2009 the Obama administration allocated $125 million to USAID to purchase food aid from local and regional producers or hand out food vouchers "when our own food assistance is too far away, or when there is ample food in the market, but crisis affected households cannot afford to buy it." Hughes, "US Food Aid Contributing to Africa's Hunger?"

16. Kenny, *Getting Better*.

17. Banerjee and Duflo, *Poor Economics*.

18. Beny and Cook, "Metals or Management?"

Chapter 10

1. Soto and Murphy, "Brazil Says BRICs Offer Conditional Help to Europe."

2. Boyd, "Harvard Peso Doctor Vindicated as Chile Evades Slump."

3. CNN Politics, "President Clinton Announces Another Record Budget Surplus."

4. Cutting taxes in a recession can spur economic growth, but this was not President Bush's motivation when he spoke before Congress on February 27, 2001—nine months before the National Bureau of Economic Research, a nonpartisan organization, declared that the U.S. economy was in recession. Also, the president's speech made no mention of the words "recession," "downturn," or "slowdown."

5. De Grauwe, "The Politics of the Maastricht Convergence Criteria."

6. European Central Bank, "Press Release: Statement of the Governing Council on the ECOFIN Council Conclusions Regarding the Correction of Excessive Deficits in France and Germany."

7. *The Economist*, "Light-weight BRICs: How IMF Voting Shares Compare with Global Economic Heft."

8. Sibaja, "Brazil Willing to Help IMF with Funds for Europe."

9. Naipaul, "Our Universal Civilization."

REFERENCES

Acemoglu, Daron, Simon Johnson, and James A. Robinson. 2001. "The Colonial Origins of Comparative Development: An Empirical Investigation." *American Economic Review* 91, no. 5: 1369–1401.

Acemoglu, Daron, and James A. Robinson. 2012. *Why Nations Fail: The Origins of Power, Prosperity, and Poverty.* New York: Crown Business.

ADVFN. 2010. "Intel Company Financial Information." Available at: http://www.advfn.com/p.php?pid=financials&symbol =NASDAQ%3AINTC (accessed September 2, 2010).

Amsden, Alice H. 1989. *Asia's Next Giant: South Korea and Late Industrialization.* New York: Oxford University Press.

Aninat, Eduardo. 2000. "Chile in the 1990s: Embracing Development Opportunities." *Finance and Development* 37, no. 1 (March): 19–21.

Arslanalp, Serkan, and Peter B. Henry. 2005. "Is Debt Relief Efficient?" *Journal of Finance* 60: 1017–1051.

———. 2006. "Helping the Poor to Help Themselves: Debt Relief or Aid?" In *Sovereign Debt at the Crossroads: Challenges and Proposals for Resolving the Third World Debt Crisis,* edited by Chris Jochnick and Fraser A. Preston. New York: Oxford University Press.

———. 2006. "Policy Watch: Debt Relief." *Journal of Economic Perspectives* 20: 207–220.

Baker, James A., III. 1995. Statement before the joint annual meetings of the International Monetary Fund and the World Bank. Seoul, South Korea (October 8).

Banerjee, Abhijit Y., and Esther Duflo. 2011. *Poor Economics: A Radical Rethinking of the Way to Fight Global Poverty.* New York: Public Affairs.

Beny, Laura N., and Lisa D. Cook. 2009. "Metals or Management? Explaining Africa's Recent Economic Growth Performance." *American Economic Review* 99: 268–274.

Bertram, Arnold. 2006. "Revisiting Michael Manley's Social Revolution." *Jamaica Gleaner*, April 9.

Bhagwati, Jagdish N. 1998. "The Capital Myth: The Difference Between Trade in Widgets and Dollars." *Foreign Affairs* 77: 7–12.

Biggs, Alan. 2010. "Electronics: A Mainstay of Korean Economy." *Korea Times*, August 25.

Blanchard, Olivier, and Carlo Cotarelli. 2010. "Ten Commandments for Fiscal Adjustment in Advanced Economies." iMFdirect, June 24. Available at: http://blog-imfdirect.imf.org/2010/06/24/ten-commandments-for-fiscal-adjustment-in-advanced-economies (accessed October 9, 2012).

Bosworth, Barry P., and Susan M. Collins. 2003. "The Empirics of Growth: An Update." *Brookings Papers on Economic Activity* 2: 113–179.

Bottelier, Pieter. 2006. "China and the World Bank: How a Partnership Was Built." Working Paper 277. Stanford, CA: Stanford Center for International Development (April).

Boyd, Sebastian. 2009. "Harvard Peso Doctor Vindicated as Chile Evades Slump." Bloomberg, April 23. Available at: http://www.bloomberg.com/apps/news?pid=newsarchive&sid=a4x4oWkXE9yM (accessed October 9, 2012).

Broad, Robin. 1987. "How About a Real Solution to Third World Debt?" *New York Times*, September 28.

Bruno, Michael, and William Easterly. 1998. "Inflation Crises and Long-Run Growth." *Journal of Monetary Economics* 41: 3–26.

Bulow, Jeremy I. 2002. "First World Governments and Third World Debt." *Brookings Papers on Economic Activity* 1: 229–255.

Carnegy, Hugh. 2012. "Germany Must Accept Growth Pact Says Hollande." *Financial Times,* April 25.

Chari, Anusha, Peter B. Henry, and Diego Sasson. 2012. "Capital Market Integration and Wages." *American Economic Journal: Macroeconomics* 42: 102–132.

Chari, Anusha, Paige P. Ouimet, and Linda L. Tesar. 2004. "Acquiring Control in Emerging Markets: Evidence from the Stock Market." Working Paper 10872. Cambridge, MA: National Bureau of Economic Research (September).

Chavez, Hugo. 2005. Speech delivered to the United Nations. New York (September 16).

CNN Money. 2011. "Procter & Gamble: Fortune 500 Rankings 2011." Available at: http://money.cnn.com/magazines/fortune/fortune500/2011/snapshots/334.html (accessed October 9, 2012).

CNN Politics. 2000. "President Clinton Announces Another Record Budget Surplus." September 27. Available at: http://articles.cnn.com/2000-09-27/politics/clinton.surplus_1_budget-surplus-national-debt-fiscal-discipline?_s=PM:ALLPOLITICS (accessed October 9, 2012).

Corbo, Vittorio. 2005. "Monetary Policy and Central Bank Independence in Chile." Paper presented at the Banco de México conference, Mexico City (November 14–15).

Corbo, Vittorio, and Stanley Fischer. 1995. "Structural Adjustment, Stabilization, and Policy Reform: Domestic and International Finance." In *Handbook of Development Economics* 3, edited by Jere Behrman and T. N. Srinivasan. Amsterdam: Elsevier.

Cowell, Alan, and Nicholas Kulish. 2012. "Austerity Faces Sharper Debate After European Elections." *New York Times,* May 7.

De Grauwe, Paul. 2009. "The Politics of the Maastricht Convergence Criteria." Vox, April 15. Available at: http://voxeu.org/article/politics-maastricht-convergence-criteria (accessed October 9, 2012).

Dernberger, Robert F. 1966. "Economic Realities." *Bulletin of the Atomic Scientists* 22 (June): 6–10.

Dornbusch, Rudiger. 1992. "The Case for Trade Liberalization in Developing Countries." *Journal of Economic Perspectives* 6: 69–85.

Easterly, William. 2003. "Can Foreign Aid Buy Growth?" *Journal of Economic Perspectives* 17: 23–48.

Eaton, Jonathan, and Mark Gersovitz. 1981. "Debt with Potential Repudiation: Theoretical and Empirical Analysis." *Review of Economic Studies* 48: 289–309.

The Economist. 2011. "Light-weight BRICS: How IMF Voting Shares Compare with Global Economic Heft." June 6. Available at: http://www.economist.com/blogs/dailychart/2011/06/imf-influence (accessed October 9, 2012).

———. 2006. "The New Titans." In "Special Report: The World Economy." September 14.

European Central Bank. 2003. "Press Release: Statement of the Governing Council on the ECOFIN Council Conclusions Regarding the Correction of Excessive Deficits in France and Germany." November 25. Available at: http://www.ecb.int/press/pr/date/2003/html/pro31125.en.html (accessed October 9, 2012).

Fairtrade Foundation. 2010. *The Great Cotton Stitch-Up.* A Fairtrade Foundation Report (November).

Farnsworth, Clyde H. 1988. "Micro-Loans to the World's Poorest." *New York Times,* February 21.

Flock, Elizabeth. 2012. "Ngozi Okonjo-Iweala, World Bank Presidential Candidate, Says She Would Focus on Job Creation." *Washington Post,* April 9.

Forbes, Kristin J. 2007. "One Cost of the Chilean Capital Controls: Increased Financial Constraints for Smaller Traded Firms." *Journal of International Economics* 71: 294–323.

G-8 Secretariat. 1999. "G-7 Statement." June 18. Available at: http://
www.g8.utoronto.ca/summit/1999koln/g7statement_june18.htm
(accessed August 16, 2012).

G-24 Secretariat. 2003. Briefing paper on the Heavily Indebted Poor
Country (HIPC) Initiative. March. Available at: http://www.g24
.org/ResearchPaps/hipc.pdf (accessed August 16, 2012).

Gil Díaz, Francisco. 2003. "Don't Blame Our Failures on Reforms
That Have Not Taken Place." *Fraser Forum* (June): 7–10.

Global Trade Alert (GTA). 2010. *Tensions Contained . . . For Now:
The 8th GTA Report.* London: Centre for Economic Policy
Research (November). Available at: http://www.globaltradealert
.org/sites/default/files/GTA8_0.pdf (accessed August 16, 2012).

Hall, Robert E., and Charles I. Jones. 1999. "Why Do Some
Countries Produce So Much More Output per Worker Than
Others?" *Quarterly Journal of Economics* 114: 83–116.

Helpman, Elhanan, and Paul Krugman. 1985. *Market Structure and
Foreign Trade.* Cambridge, MA: MIT Press.

Henry, Peter B. 2000. "Stock Market Liberalization, Economic
Reform, and Emerging Market Equity Prices." *Journal of Finance*
55: 529–564.

———. 2002. "Is Disinflation Good for the Stock Market?" *Journal of
Finance* 57: 1617–1648.

———. 2003. "Capital Account Liberalization, the Cost of Capital,
and Economic Growth." *American Economic Review* 93: 91–96.

———. 2007. "Capital Account Liberalization: Theory, Evidence,
and Speculation." *Journal of Economic Literature* 45: 887–935.

———. 2008. Testimony before the Senate Committee on Foreign
Relations. April 24. Available at: http://www.foreign.senate.gov
/imo/media/doc/HenryTestimony
080424p.pdf (accessed August 16, 2012).

Henry, Peter B., and Prakash Kannan. 2008. "Growth and Returns in
Emerging Markets." In *International Financial Issues in the Pacific
Rim: Global Imbalances, Financial Liberalization, and Exchange*

Rate Policy, edited by Takatoshi Ito and Andrew Rose. Chicago: University of Chicago Press.

Henry, Peter B., and Peter L. Lorentzen. 2003. "Domestic Capital Market Reform and Access to Global Finance: Making Markets Work." In *The Future of Domestic Capital Markets in Developing Countries,* edited by Robert E. Litan, Michael Pomerleano, and V. Sundararajan. Washington, DC: Brookings Institution Press.

Henry, Peter B., and Conrad Miller. 2009. "Institutions vs. Policies: A Tale of Two Islands." *American Economic Review* 99: 261–267.

Holderith, Robert C. 2011. "The Myth of Developed Market Multinationals as Emerging Market Investment Surrogates." Emerging Global Advisors (November). Available at: http://www .emergingglobaladvisors.com/pdf/EGA%20Commentary%20Nov ember%202011%20Final.pdf (accessed August 16, 2012).

Hughes, Dana. 2009. "US Food Aid Contributing to Africa's Hunger?" *ABC World News with Diane Sawyer,* October 29. Available at: http://abcnews.go.com/WN/Health/us-food-aid -contributing-africas-hunger/story?id=8939151#.UC63yiN Wr2B (accessed August 17, 2012).

International Monetary Fund (IMF). 2010. *World Economic Outlook: Rebalancing Growth.* Washington, DC: IMF (April).

———. 2010. "United Republic of Tanzania: Financial System Stability Assessment Update." IMF Country Report 10/177 (June). Available at: http://www.imf.org/external/pubs/ft/scr/ 2010/cr10177.pdf (accessed July 19, 2012).

———. 2011. "Quota and Voting Shares Before and After Implementation of Reforms Agreed in 2008 and 2010." Available at: http://www.imf.org/external/np/sec/pr/2011/pdfs/ quota_tbl.pdf (accessed August 16, 2012).

———. 2012. "Factsheet: The IMF's Flexible Credit Line (FCL)." April 18. Available at: http://www.imf.org/external/np/exr/facts /fcl.htm (accessed August 16, 2012).

Kaminsky, Graciela, and Carmen Reinhart. 1999. "The Twin Crises: Causes of Banking and Balance of Payments Problems." *American Economic Review* 89, no. 3: 473–500.

Kanaan, Oussama. 2000. "Tanzania's Experience with Trade Liberalization." *Trade and Development* (June): 30–33.

Kelkar, Vijay. 1999. "India's Emerging Economic Challenges." *Economic and Political Weekly* 34: 2326–2329.

Kenny, Charles. 2011. *Getting Better: Why Global Development Is Succeeding—And How We Can Improve the World Even More.* New York: Basic Books.

Kim, Linsu. 1999. *Learning and Innovation in Economic Development.* Northampton, MA: Edward Elgar Publishing.

———. 2003. "The Dynamics of Technology Development: Lessons from the Korean Experience." In *Competitiveness, FDI, and Technological Activity in East Asia,* edited by Sanjaya Lall and Shujiro Urata. Northampton, MA: Edward Elgar Publishing.

Kindleberger, Charles. 1978. *Manias, Panics, and Crashes.* New York: Basic Books.

Kotkin, Stephen. 2007. "First World, Third World (Maybe Not in That Order)." *New York Times,* May 6.

Krueger, Anne O. 1995. "East Asian Growth Experience and Endogenous Growth Theory." In *Growth Theories in Light of the East Asian Experience,* edited by Takatoshi Ito and Anne O. Krueger. National Bureau of Economic Research East Asia Seminar on Economics. Chicago: University of Chicago Press.

———. 2004. "Meant Well, Tried Little, Failed Much: Policy Reforms in Emerging Market Economies." Roundtable lecture presented at the Economic Honors Society, New York University, New York (March 23).

———. 2009. "Trade Liberalization and Growth in Developing Countries." Paper presented at the American Economic Association meeting, New Orleans (January 4–6).

Krugman, Paul. 1988. "Financing vs. Forgiving a Debt Overhang."
    Working Paper 2486. Cambridge, MA: National Bureau of
    Economic Research (January).

La Porta, Rafael, Florencio Lopez-de-Silanes, and Andrei Shleifer.
    2008. "The Economic Consequences of Legal Origins." *Journal of
    Economic Literature* 46: 285–332.

La Porta, Rafael, Florencio Lopez-de-Silanes, Andrei Shleifer, and
    Robert W. Vishny. 1997. "Legal Determinants of External
    Finance." *Journal of Finance* 52: 1131–1150.

———. 1998. "Law and Finance." *Journal of Political Economy* 106:
    1113–1155.

———. 2002. "Investor Protection and Corporate Valuation." *Journal
    of Finance* 57: 1147–1170.

Levi, Darrell E. 1990. *Michael Manley: The Making of a Leader.*
    Athens: University of Georgia Press.

Levitt, Kari. 2005. *Reclaiming Development: Independent Thought and
    the Caribbean Community.* Kingston, Jamaica: Ian Randle
    Publishers.

Lora, Eduardo, Ugo Panizza, and Myriam Quispe-Agnoli. 2003.
    "Reform Fatigue: Symptoms, Reasons, Implications." Paper
    presented at the conference "Rethinking Structural Reform in
    Latin America," Federal Reserve Bank of Atlanta (October 23).

MacKinlay, A. Craig. 1997. "Event Studies in Economics and
    Finance." *Journal of Economic Literature* 35, no. 1: 13–39.

Martell, Rodolfo, and René M. Stulz. 2003. "Equity-Market
    Liberalizations as Country IPOs." *American Economic Review* 93:
    97–101.

Massaquoi, Hans J. 1990. "*Ebony* Interview with Jamaica Prime
    Minister Michael Manley." *Ebony* (February): 110–118.

Murphy, Sophia, and Kathy McAfee. 2005. *US Food Aid: Time to Get
    It Right.* Minneapolis: Institute for Agriculture and Trade Policy
    (July).

Mwasalwiba, Ernest, Heidi Dahles, and Ingrid Wakkee. 2012. "Graduate Entrepreneurship in Tanzania: Contextual Enablers and Hindrances." *European Journal of Scientific Research* 76: 386–402.

Naím, Moisés. 2000. "Washington Consensus or Washington Confusion?" *Foreign Policy* (Spring): 87–103.

Naipaul, V. S. 1990. "Our Universal Civilization." Walter B. Wriston Lecture (October 30).

Nessman, Ravi. 2012. "Indian Strike Against Reforms Shuts Trains, Shops." Associated Press, September 20. Available at: http://bigstory.ap.org/article/opposition-led-strike-hits-trains-india (accessed September 30, 2012).

Noonan, Peggy. 2011. "This Is No Time for Moderation." *Wall Street Journal,* October 15.

Obstfeld, Maurice. 1998. "The Global Capital Market: Benefactor or Menace?" *Journal of Economic Perspectives* 12: 9–30.

O'Neil, Jim, Dominic Wilson, Roopa Purushothaman, and Anna Stupnytska. 2005. "How Solid Are the BRICs?" Goldman Sachs Global Economics Paper 134 (December 1).

Organization for Economic Cooperation and Development (OECD). 2008. *OECD Benchmark Definition of Foreign Direct Investment,* 4th ed. Available at: http://www.oecd.org/dataoecd/26/50/40193734.pdf (accessed August 16, 2012).

Palmer, Doug, and Catherine Bosley. 2012. "IMF Shows New Flexibility on Fiscal Austerity." Reuters, May 7. Available at: http://www.reuters.com/article/2012/05/07/us-imf-lagarde-idUSBRE84615920120507 (accessed October 9, 2012).

Payne, Anthony J. 1988. *Politics in Jamaica.* London: C. Hurst & Co.

Pregelj, Vladimir N. 2001. "Most-Favored-Nation Trade Status of the People's Republic of China." Report for the Library of Congress. Washington, DC: Congressional Research Service (June). Available at: http://www.au.af.mil/au/awc/awcgate/crs/rl30225.pdf (accessed August 16, 2012).

Reagan, Ronald W. 1986. "Remarks to Employees of the Department of the Treasury." February 5.

Reed, Lawrence W. 1988. "Hyperinflation Threatens Brazil." *The Freeman* 38, no. 1 (January).

Reinhart, Carmen M., and Kenneth S. Rogoff. 2009. *This Time Is Different: Eight Centuries of Financial Folly.* Princeton, NJ: Princeton University Press.

Risager, Ole. 1995. "On the Effects of Trade Policy Reform: The Case of Jordan." University of Copenhagen Economic Policy Research Unit Working Paper Series 95–16.

Robotham, Don. 2003. "Learning from Barbados." *Jamaica Gleaner,* February 2.

Rodríguez, Francisco, and Dani Rodrik. 2000. "Trade Policy and Economic Growth: A Skeptic's Guide to the Cross-National Evidence." May. Available at: http://www.hks.harvard.edu/fs/drodrik/Research%20papers/skepti 1299.pdf (accessed October 9, 2012).

Rodrik, Dani. 1998. "Who Needs Capital-Account Convertibility?" In *Should the IMF Pursue Capital-Account Convertibility? Essays in International Finance,* no. 207, edited by Stanley Fischer. Princeton, NJ: Princeton University, Department of Economics, International Finance Section.

———. 2006. "Goodbye Washington Consensus, Hello Washington Confusion? A Review of the World Bank's Economic Growth in the 1990s: Learning from a Decade of Reform." *Journal of Economic Literature* 44: 973–987.

Rogoff, Kenneth S. 1999. "International Institutions for Reducing Global Financial Instability." *Journal of Economic Perspectives* 13: 21–42.

Rose, Andrew K., and Mark M. Spiegel. 2002. "A Gravity Model of Sovereign Lending: Trade, Default, and Credit." Working Paper 9285. Cambridge, MA: National Bureau of Economic Research (October).

Rudolph, Barbara, Andrea Dabrowski, James L. Graff, and James O. Jackson. 1991. "A Global Fire Sale." *Time,* April 22.

Sachs, Jeffrey D. 1984. *Theoretical Issues in International Borrowing.* Princeton Studies in International Finance 54. Princeton, NJ: Princeton University Press.

———. 1986. "Managing the LDC Debt Crisis." *Brookings Papers on Economic Activity* 2: 397–440.

———. 1989. "Introduction." *Developing Country Debt and the World Economy.* Chicago: University of Chicago Press.

Sargent, Thomas. 1982. "The Ends of Four Big Inflations." In *Inflation: Causes and Consequences,* edited by Robert E. Hall. Chicago: University of Chicago Press.

Sewell, Dan. 2009. "Procter & Gamble Aims to Add 1 Billion Customers." Associated Press (last modified October 13). Available at: http://www.manufacturing.net/News-Procter-Gamble-Aims-For-1-Billion-Customers-101309.aspx (accessed August 25, 2010).

Shiller, Robert J. 2000. *Irrational Exuberance.* Princeton, NJ: Princeton University Press.

Shleifer, Andrei. 2009. "The Age of Milton Friedman." *Journal of Economic Literature* 47: 123–135.

Sibaja, Marco. 2011. "Brazil Willing to Help IMF with Funds for Europe." Associated Press, November 8.

Singapore Election 2011. "How Forced CPF Savings Help PAP to Generate 'High' Growth Rates." May 1. Available at: http://singaporege2011.wordpress.com/2011/05/01/how-forced-cpf-savings-help-pap-to-generate-high-growth-rates/ (accessed August 16, 2012).

Soto, Alonso, and Peter Murphy. 2011. "Brazil Says BRICs Offer Conditional Help to Europe." Reuters, December 2. Available at: http://in.reuters.com/article/2011/12/02/brazil-imf-europe -idINDEE7B104820111202 (accessed August 16, 2012).

Speth, James G. 1999. "Debt Relief, Yes, but Development Aid as Well." *New York Times,* May 7.

Spilimbergo, Antonio, Steve Symansky, Olivier Blanchard, and Carlo Cottarelli. 2008. "Fiscal Policy for the Crisis." IMF Staff Position Note SPN/08/01. Washington, DC: International Monetary Fund (December 29).

Stein, Herbert. 1999. *What I Think: Essays on Economics, Politics, and Life.* Washington, DC: American Enterprise Institute Press.

Stiglitz, Joseph E. 2002. *Globalization and Its Discontents.* New York: W. W. Norton.

———. 2002. "A Global Agenda for Employment." Lecture delivered at the International Labour Organization's Employment Forum. Geneva (January). Available at: http://www.ilo.org/public/english/revue/download/pdf/stiglitz.pdf (accessed August 16, 2012).

Stone, Carl, and Stanislaw Wellisz. 1993. "Jamaica." In *The Political Economy of Poverty, Equity, and Growth: Five Small Open Economies,* edited by Ronald Findlay and Stanislaw Wellisz. New York: Oxford University Press.

Surowiecki, James. 2004. *The Wisdom of Crowds: Why the Many Are Smarter Than the Few and How Collective Wisdom Shapes Business, Economies, Societies, and Nations.* New York: Doubleday.

Tanzi, Vito. 1977. "Inflation, Lags in Collection, and the Real Value of Tax Revenue." International Monetary Fund Staff Papers 24 (March): 154–167.

Thomas, Vinod. 2006. *From Inside Brazil: Development in a Land of Contrasts.* Palo Alto, CA, and Washington, DC: Stanford University Press and the World Bank.

Time. 1969. "Mining: Nationalization in Zambia." August 22.

———. 1977. "Business: IBM Withdraws from India." November 28.

Times Live. 2011. "Trevor Manuel Slams Europe's IMF Hold." Times Live (South Africa), May 24. Available at: http://www

.timeslive.co.za/local/article1082998.ece/Trevor-Manuel-slams
-Europes-IMF-hold (accessed August 16, 2012).

Twomey, Michael J. 1998. "Patterns of Foreign Investment in the
Third World in the Twentieth Century." June. Available at:
http://www-personal.umd.umich.edu/~mtwomey/fdi/Paper.pdf
(accessed August 16, 2012).

US Department of State. 2012. "Background Note: Zambia."
February 22. Available at: http://www.state.gov/r/pa/ei/bgn/
2359.htm (accessed August 16, 2012).

Vatican, The. 1998. "Bull of Indiction of the Great Jubilee of the Year
2000" (Pope John Paul II's statement on debt relief). November
29. Available at: http://www.vatican.va/jubilee_2000/docs/
documents/hf_jp-ii_doc_30111998_bolla-jubilee_en.html
(accessed August 17, 2012).

Volcker, Paul A. 1985. Remarks before the sixty-third annual meeting
of the Bankers' Association for Foreign Trade. Boca Raton, FL
(May 13).

Wacziarg, Romain, and Karen H. Welch. 2008. "Trade Liberalization
and Growth: New Evidence." *World Bank Economic Review* 22:
187–231.

Walters, Denine. 2010. "Failure of Zambia's Nationalisation
Programme: Exploring the Factors That Precipitated the
Collapse." *Consultancy Africa Intelligence* (October 17).

Wentz, Laurel. 2009. "Top 100 Global Advertisers Heap Their
Spending Abroad." Ad Age/Global (November 30). Available at:
http://adage.com/globalnews/article?article_id=140723 (accessed
August 26, 2010).

Wheat, Andrew. 1995. "The Fall of the Peso and the Mexican
'Miracle.'" *Multinational Monitor*. Available at: http://www
.multinationalmonitor.org/hyper/issues/1995/04/mm0495
_06.html (accessed July 21, 2010).

Williamson, John. 1989. "What Washington Means by Policy
Reform." In *Latin American Readjustment: How Much Has*

Happened, edited by John Williamson. Washington, DC: Institute for International Economics.

———. 2002. Speech delivered at the Center for Strategic and International Studies. Washington, DC (November 6).

Wilson, Dominic, and Roopa Purushothaman. 2003. "Dreaming with BRICs: The Path to 2050." Goldman Sachs Global Economics Paper 99 (October 1).

Wint, Alvin G. 2003. *Competitiveness in Small Developing Economies: Insights from the Caribbean.* Kingston, Jamaica: University of the West Indies Press.

World Bank. 2005. "Something Special About the 1990s?" In *Economic Growth in the 1990s: Learning from a Decade of Reform.* Washington, DC: World Bank.

———. 2009. "World Development Indicators, 2009." Washington, DC: World Bank. Available at: http://data.worldbank.org/data-catalog/world-development-indicators (accessed August 16, 2012).

Yergin, Daniel, and Joseph Stanislaw. 2002. *The Commanding Heights: The Battle for the World Economy.* New York: Free Press.

INDEX